WITHDRAWN

P. ALLEN SMITH'S
SEASONAL RECIPES FROM THE GARDEN

P. ALLEN SMITH'S
SEASONAL RECIPES FROM THE GARDEN

P. ALLEN SMITH

PHOTOGRAPHS BY BEN FINK

Clarkson Potter/Publishers
New York

Copyright © 2010 by Hortus, Ltd.
Photographs copyright © 2010 by Ben Fink, except pages
6, 7, 14, 47, 56, 58, 73, 96, 115, 125, 129, 134, 135, 152,
153, 172, 177, 185, 187, 188, 209, 228, 244, which are
copyright © 2010 by Hortus, Ltd.

Published in the United States by Clarkson Potter/Publishers, an
imprint of the Crown Publishing Group, a division of Random
House, Inc., New York.
www.crownpublishing.com
www.clarksonpotter.com

CLARKSON POTTER is a trademark and POTTER with colophon
is a registered trademark of Random House, Inc.

Library of Congress Cataloging-in-Publication Data
Smith, P. Allen.
[Seasonal recipes from the garden]
P. Allen Smith's seasonal recipes from the garden / P. Allen Smith.
— 1st ed.
    1. Cookery. 2. Cookery (Vegetables) 3. Cookery (Fruit).
I. Title. II. Title: Seasonal recipes from the garden.
TX714.S592 2010
641.5—dc22   2009049730

ISBN 978-0-307-35108-1

Printed in China

Design by Stephanie Huntwork
Jacket photographs © 2010 by Ben Fink
Photographs on pages 11–13 from the author's collection

10 9 8 7 6 5 4 3 2 1

First Edition

To
AUNT GENNY and TERI
for all the good times and
great food
shared in the kitchen

Contents

Summer

Fall

Winter

INTRODUCTION

WHEN I FIRST ENTERTAINED THE IDEA of creating a cookbook for my Garden Home series, it felt right. After all, I've been featuring cooking segments in my television shows and on my web site for years. I couldn't pass up the chance to combine two of my favorite activities: gardening and eating! It's been fun to assemble a fresh assortment of recipes for this book. The most challenging part was narrowing the selections—there are so many delicious ways to make a meal.

In my first book, *The Garden Home,* and in those that followed, I illustrated ways to blend the comforts of home with the beauty of the garden to create welcoming and stylish living areas. Growing garden-fresh produce to use in home-cooked meals is an extension of that idea. One of the greatest pleasures of living in a Garden Home is having herbs, fruits, and vegetables just steps from your kitchen, ready to use in your favorite recipes. This cookbook offers information about gardening and shopping for local produce so you can experience the delicious difference it makes in your meals. My hope is that it will also serve to reinforce the connection between what you eat and where it is grown.

Now, that's not a new idea. It springs directly from one of Thomas Jefferson's founding principles for this country. He believed that the closer people were to the land, the freer they were to experience their lives and embrace their rights. This notion took hold just as the first states were being established and the role of the farmer took on a new, elevated status. Jefferson described noble cultivators, or "yeomen farmers," as enlightened citizens trained in many fields, and therefore the group most capable of guiding the development of our young country. In the 1790s, 90 percent of the workforce was engaged in farming and many of the country's leaders, including Jefferson, were farmers. In fact, gardening was one of his greatest joys. He wrote: "No occupation is so delightful to me as the culture of the earth and no culture comparable to that of the garden."

I have experienced that same enduring pleasure that Jefferson described, and it's the reason I chose a career as a garden designer. I'm often asked how I moved from my family's garden center to demonstrating gardening ideas on national television. It all started when I realized how many people had lost the connection to their families' agrarian past. As a child who grew up on family farms where most of the food on the table was garden-grown and our livelihood came from the crops in the fields, I was surprised when I encountered so many people who longed to have a garden but needed some basic information on how to start. To help introduce them to the joys of gardening, I started going on TV and radio programs to answer their questions and give them some how-to advice.

Happily, we seem to be reconnecting to the garden and the idea that eating food grown close to home is best for ourselves, our communities, and the Earth. And every day there are more ways to enjoy fresh locally grown produce, such as farmers' markets, food cooperatives, and community-supported agriculture, in addition to the produce you can grow yourself. And there is no better way to explore the pleasure of local food than by cooking up some great meals. By celebrating diversity, locally grown, organic, in season, we are taking another look at the food we are eating and experiencing it more the way our forebears did not so long ago. We are taking part in a new era that encourages the idea of New American cooking.

These dishes come from several sources; many are my family's favorites, others were inspired by meals I've enjoyed with friends, and a few came from chefs who agreed to share their recipes after I experienced memorable meals in their restaurants. All the recipes have been home-tested and tasted in my kitchen—a project I thoroughly enjoyed! As I sampled and adjusted the ingredients, it was amazing how the aromas stirred up all kinds of memories and transported me back to earlier days. Many of the stories I share in the book came to me while I was savoring the flavors of these dishes.

One of my greatest culinary joys is preparing food that is matched to the season. Fresh fruits and vegetables just seem to go with the time of year when they are ready for harvest. It's hard to imagine eating stick-to-your-ribs winter squash on a hot summer day or snacking on a bowl of chilled cantaloupe while watching the first snowfall. So the recipes are arranged by the season when their ingredients are at their garden-fresh best.

Along with the 120-plus seasonal recipes, I've included a short how-to guide about the food I grow and some simple ideas on how you can do the same. You'll be surprised at all the produce that can be grown in a small space. I also share a list of my favorite garden varieties so you can enjoy four seasons of good eating. It is such a rich experience—I hope you'll give it a try. Julia Child often exalted, *"Bon appétit!"* I offer my own version, as a cook and gardener: *"Dig in!"*

LEFT Aunt Genny Womak bringing jars of garden vegetables from the cellar to the kitchen.

LEFT Great Uncle Clark Edward Smith in the garden, Dark Hollow, Tennessee.

BELOW LEFT Aunt Genny Womack with Robert Allen Smith's mules, Queenie and Belle, Warren County, Tennessee.

BELOW Paul Allen Smith Sr., age twelve, Warren County, Tennessee.

BOTTOM Josephine Foster (far right) with cousins in her kitchen, Thanksgiving, 1938, Lonoke County, Arkansas.

TOP LEFT Great Uncle Clark Edward Smith with mules next to the vegetable garden in Dark Hollow, Tennessee.

TOP RIGHT Mary Bina Hillis Smith (left) with her older sister Permelia Elizabeth Hillis Jones, also known as "Aunt Lizzie."

ABOVE LEFT George Washington and Mary Hillis Smith's (my great-grandparents) house, 1930, Dark Hollow, Tennessee.

ABOVE Uncle Tom Russell, Paul Allen Smith Sr., Aunt Genny Womack, Uncle Lyndon Smith, and Uncle Ted Smith with the pet dogs and goat.

LEFT Aunt Genny Womack with her grandchildren in the vegetable garden, 1982.

SPRING

STRAWBERRY LEMONADE

EVERYONE SEEMS TO LOVE STRAWBERRIES. In fact, I've never met anyone who passes them up! They are so lovely and sweet—particularly berries that are locally grown. In my garden, I have three varieties: 'Cardinal', 'Ozark Beauty', and 'AllStar'. They are all ruby-red jewels of pure pleasure. Pop one in your mouth and a pleasant, light aroma travels up your throat to your nose, before it even gets to your tongue. Sink your teeth into the fruit, and the tiny outer seeds offer a subtle crunch as the flavor of spring sunshine fills your mouth.

Garden varieties are grown for their taste, while their big, watery supermarket cousins are selected for their size (and are often hollow inside) and their ability to be shipped long distances and then sit in a produce aisle for days, seemingly unchanged. Once you've had the chance to make a taste comparison between the two, there is no going back; you'll be scouting out U-Pick-'Em farms and farmers' markets or will try your hand at growing a patch yourself.

I can't help but pop the sweet fruits right into my mouth as I harvest them, and I enjoy them in many recipes. This strawberry lemonade combination tastes like pure nectar and is a favorite of all age groups. When the berries are ripe, this is the drink of the house.

SERVES 6

2 cups water

1½ cups sugar

1 tablespoon grated lemon zest

1 cup fresh lemon juice

1 pint fresh strawberries, hulled and halved

2 cups chilled sparkling water or club soda

Ice

Fresh mint sprigs, for garnish

Whole strawberries, for garnish

Combine the water and sugar in a medium saucepan and bring to a boil. Once the mixture is bubbling, reduce the heat and simmer, stirring occasionally, until the sugar has dissolved. Add the lemon zest and juice, stir, and then remove the pan from the heat. Let the mixture cool completely, and then pour it through a strainer into a clean pitcher.

Puree the pint of strawberries in a blender and add the puree to the lemonade. Stir well to combine, and refrigerate until nice and cold.

Just before serving, add the chilled sparkling water and stir well. Pour into glasses filled with ice, garnish each one with a mint sprig and a strawberry, and serve.

CHICKEN KEBOBS STAVROS

SERVES 6

12 6-inch bamboo
    skewers

FOR THE CHICKEN

¼ cup olive oil

6 garlic cloves, chopped

2 tablespoons finely
    chopped fresh mint
    leaves, or 2 teaspoons
    dried

2 tablespoons finely
    chopped fresh
    oregano leaves, or
    2 teaspoons dried

½ teaspoon kosher salt

½ teaspoon freshly
    ground black pepper

3 pounds skinless,
    boneless chicken
    breasts and thighs,
    cut into 1-inch pieces

FOR THE KEBOBS

1 red onion, cut into
    1-inch pieces

Large fresh mint leaves

Salt and freshly ground
    black pepper, to taste

2 tablespoons olive oil

2 tablespoons fresh
    lemon juice

Greek Salad (recipe
    follows)

I'M NOTORIOUS FOR GOING STRAIGHT into a restaurant kitchen to talk to the chef. One of my favorite local dining haunts is a great restaurant called Trio's, in Little Rock, Arkansas. When I tried these chicken kebobs, I knew I'd be after chef Capi Peck Peterson for the ingredients. It's a great appetizer and can be served with a classic Greek salad.

In a large bowl, mix the olive oil, garlic, mint, oregano, salt, and pepper together. Then add the pieces of chicken, and stir to coat. Let the meat marinate for 30 minutes or longer.

While the chicken is marinating, soak the skewers in cold water.

Preheat an outdoor grill or the broiler.

To assemble the kebobs, alternate pieces of chicken with pieces of onion and mint leaves on each skewer. Sprinkle with salt and pepper, and set aside.

Whisk the olive oil and lemon juice together in a small bowl, and set it aside.

Arrange the kebobs 3 inches from the heat, and grill, turning the skewers and basting them with the lemon–olive oil mixture several times, until the chicken is cooked through, 5 to 8 minutes.

To serve, crisscross two skewers on a small plate, and serve with 1 cup of the Greek Salad.

GREEK SALAD
MAKES 6 CUPS (1 CUP PER SERVING)

2½ cups cored and coarsely chopped fresh tomatoes

2½ cups peeled and coarsely chopped English (seedless) cucumber

½ cup diced red bell pepper

½ cup pitted kalamata olives, cut in half

½ cup finely diced red onion

5 tablespoons chopped fresh parsley leaves

¼ cup olive oil

2 tablespoons red wine vinegar

1 teaspoon finely chopped fresh oregano leaves, or ½ teaspoon dried

Crumbled feta cheese, to taste

In a large serving bowl, toss all the ingredients together except for the feta. Just before serving, gently mix in the feta.

SMOKED BLUE CAT PÂTÉ

MAKES 2 CUPS

8 ounces boneless, skinless catfish fillets (about 2 fillets)

2 to 4 teaspoons Allen's Seafood Rub (recipe follows)

1 8-ounce package cream cheese, at room temperature

¼ cup good-quality mayonnaise (such as Hellmann's)

¼ cup fresh lemon juice

¼ cup sliced green onions, white and green parts

1 teaspoon liquid hickory smoke flavoring (see Note)

Crackers or toast rounds, for serving

"TRY IT—YOU'LL LIKE IT" is the encouragement I'd give to anyone considering this recipe. It is a delicious, easy-to-whip-up Southern hors d'oeuvre that has been awarded top honors at international food shows. Catfish is a nonthreatened species of fish that is farm-raised. With its white flaky flesh and nonfishy taste, it is very versatile. Now, that may be surprising to those who think of catfish more as a staple of the Friday-night fish fry, featuring fillets dredged in seasoned cornmeal and deep-fried in oil, accompanied by tartar sauce, pickles, coleslaw, and fries. This catfish spread has a decidedly different taste, with a subtle blend of smoky flavors mixed with the bite of fresh green onions and the zip of lemon.

Prepare an indoor or outdoor smoker to cook fish. (I use an outdoor smoker with charcoal briquettes and hickory wood chips.)

Rub each catfish fillet with 1 to 2 teaspoons of the seafood rub. Smoke the fillets, following the manufacturer's guidelines for your smoker, until the fish is cooked completely and flakes with a fork, approximately 45 minutes.

In the bowl of a food processor, combine the smoked catfish, cream cheese, mayonnaise, lemon juice, green onions, and liquid smoke. Process until the mixture is smooth and creamy, about the consistency of peanut butter. Refrigerate until serving time.

Serve with assorted crackers or toast rounds.

NOTE: Bottled liquid smoke can be found in the condiment or seasoning section of most grocery stores. I used Colgin Liquid Smoke with natural hickory flavor.

ALLEN'S SEAFOOD RUB
MAKES 4 TEASPOONS

1 teaspoon ground white pepper	1 teaspoon dried parsley flakes	1 teaspoon dried thyme leaves
1 teaspoon salt		

Stir all the ingredients together thoroughly in a small bowl.

CHILLED PEA SOUP WITH BACON AND WHIPPED CREAM

SERVES 6

AMONG THE MORE THAN 330 VEGETABLE varieties that Thomas Jefferson grew in his 1,000-foot terraced garden at Monticello was the English pea, which many believe to have been his favorite. Jefferson grew fifteen types of peas, and in his 1819 garden diary, he noted with apparent delight the happy occasion when "peas come to table." To enjoy these tasty legumes for as many weeks as possible, Jefferson staggered plantings through the spring so he was able to dine on garden-fresh peas from the middle of May to the middle of July.

One of the reasons that Jefferson so gleefully noted when the peas were ready may have had to do with a friendly competition he had with several of his neighbors: whoever could produce the first peas of spring would host the others for dinner and proudly serve them as the featured dish. One local farmer, George Divers, almost always won. But one year, the story goes, Jefferson actually had the first peas, but he knew Divers took such pride in being the first that he kept news of the earlier harvest to himself. When Jefferson was urged to take his rightful place as host of the first pea dinner, he said, "No, say nothing about it. It will be more agreeable to our friend to think that he never fails."

Here in Arkansas, I usually try my best to have the seeds planted before Valentine's Day. The earlier the start, the more abundantly they produce because they thrive in the cool, wet weather of spring. It is such fun to push those fat, robust seeds into the cold ground, knowing that in just ten days they will defy the frost and begin to emerge.

This recipe for pea soup comes from talented chef Lee Richardson, who masterfully orchestrates a creative menu for Ashley's, the historic Capital Hotel's restaurant in Little Rock. Chef Richardson uses my organically grown produce, including peas, in his restaurant.

1 cup heavy cream
1 teaspoon salt
4 ounces thick-sliced bacon
½ onion, finely diced
6 cups chicken broth
½ teaspoon ground white pepper
2 pounds shelled fresh English peas, or 2 pounds frozen English peas, thawed
Fresh pea tendrils, immature pea pods, or mint leaves, for garnish (optional)

recipe continues

In a small mixing bowl, beat the heavy cream with a pinch of the salt until it forms soft peaks. Keep the whipped cream in the refrigerator until ready to serve.

Cut the bacon into large pieces, and cook them slowly in a saucepan over medium heat until crispy. Remove the bacon from the drippings, and let the pieces drain on paper towels.

Add the diced onions to the bacon drippings in the pan, and cook over medium heat until the onions become translucent, about 5 minutes. Then add the broth, the rest of the salt, and the white pepper and bring to a boil. Add the peas and cook for approximately 1 minute, or until they become bright green. Transfer the mixture, a small portion at a time, to a blender and puree until liquefied. Fill a large bowl with ice and cold water. Pour the pea soup into a smaller bowl, set it in the ice bath, and let it chill completely. Then adjust the seasoning to taste.

Ladle the chilled soup into individual bowls, and add a dollop of the whipped cream and a sprinkling of the cooked bacon to each one. Garnish the soup with fresh pea tendrils, tiny pea pods, or a leaf or two of mint, and serve.

What's In a Name?

The peas in this recipe are the small round peas in tubular pods—the kind that are shelled. They are called green peas, English peas, garden peas, or shelled peas. Flat edible pea pods are called Chinese peas or snow peas. Tube-shaped edible pods are called sugar snap peas.

WATERCRESS SOUP

THIS SOUP IS A LIGHT, welcome addition to any dinner party. Use your most delicate soup bowls or cups to match the fine flavor.

Watercress is a quintessential plant of spring; its fresh, crunchy flavor captures the taste of the season. It will grow quite happily in very moist soil—or even in a bucket of water! It's easy to grow from seed for harvesting year-round, and you can find it in most farmers' markets and produce sections. I grow it in long narrow trays placed in the kitchen windowsills during the winter and early spring.

The soup can be made a day or two ahead and stored in the refrigerator.

SERVES 6

1 pound watercress

4 tablespoons (½ stick) butter

¼ cup olive oil

1 large sweet onion, chopped

1 garlic clove, minced

1 large potato (8 ounces), peeled and diced

1 teaspoon salt

½ teaspoon freshly ground black pepper

1½ cups water

1 cup milk

1¼ cups chicken broth

1 cup half-and-half

2 large egg yolks, at room temperature

2 tablespoons walnut oil

Reserve several watercress sprigs for garnish. Chop the remaining watercress, and set it aside.

Heat the butter and olive oil in a medium saucepan over medium heat. Add the onions and sauté until they are translucent, about 5 minutes. Then add the minced garlic and sauté for a minute or so. Add the potatoes, salt, pepper, and water, and bring to a boil. Reduce the heat and simmer until the potatoes are tender, about 10 to 14 minutes.

Add the chopped watercress to the potato mixture. Stir in the milk and chicken broth, and simmer for 15 minutes.

In small batches, puree the mixture in a food processor or blender, and then return it to the pan.

Whisk the half-and-half and egg yolks together in a small bowl, and add the mixture to the soup. Heat the soup slowly, without boiling, until it thickens, about 5 minutes.

Serve the soup either hot or cold. Garnish each serving with watercress sprigs, and drizzle each one with 1 teaspoon of the walnut oil.

Watercress is a perennial plant that grows best in a moderately cool climate. Thinly broadcast seeds over finely prepared potting mix and lightly rake to cover the seeds. Keep them damp and at approximately 60°F; the seeds will germinate in about 10 days. When seedlings are 2 inches high, transplant them into a water-covered bed in full sun. As your plants grow, continue to raise the water level accordingly.

GRILLED SALMON SANDWICH WITH LEMON-DILL MAYO

SERVES 4

LEMON-DILL MAYO

1½ cups good-quality mayonnaise (such as Hellmann's)

Grated zest and juice of 2 lemons

2 tablespoons chopped fresh dill leaves

4 wild Alaskan salmon fillets (about 4 ounces each)

8 slices bakery sandwich bread (each about ½ inch thick)

Olive oil to brush on the bread

1 medium cucumber, peeled and seeded, halved lengthwise, and cut into ⅛-inch-thick slices

2 tomatoes, cored and sliced

Fresh arugula leaves, rinsed thoroughly and patted dry

1 red onion, sliced into thin rings

Sea salt and freshly ground black pepper

I ADORE THE FLAVOR OF GRILLED SALMON. This sandwich combines that wonderfully smoky salmon taste with some garden-fresh vegetables to make an easy, sensational meal. The salmon is brightened with a topping of fresh dill sauce and the spice of peppery arugula leaves, along with some first-of-the-season tomatoes and cucumbers. Toasting the bread along with the salmon gives the sandwich some added texture.

Preheat an outdoor grill.

Mix the mayo ingredients together in a small bowl, and then divide it in half. Set aside one portion to spread on the toast after the salmon is grilled. Rub both sides of the salmon fillets with the remaining Lemon-Dill Mayo.

Just before you put the fillets on the grill, place the bread slices on a baking sheet and brush them on both sides with olive oil. Transfer the bread to the grill. Then lay the fillets on the grill and cook them for 2 to 3 minutes on each side, until the fish is cooked completely and flakes with a fork. Remove the fillets from the grill and set them aside. Remove the bread when it is toasted on both sides.

To assemble the sandwiches, spread the reserved Lemon-Dill Mayo over the toasted bread slices. Place a salmon fillet on each of four slices. Top with the cucumbers, tomato slices, arugula, and red onion rings, and season with sea salt and black pepper to taste. Place the remaining toasted bread slices on top, cut each sandwich in half diagonally, and serve immediately.

RADISH AND PEPPER SANDWICH WITH POPPY SEED SPREAD

SERVES 4

POPPY SEED SPREAD

½ cup room-
   temperature cream
   cheese, mayonnaise,
   or thick yogurt

1½ teaspoon poppy
   seeds

1 teaspoon grated
   lemon zest

2 tablespoons fresh
   lemon juice

Pinch of salt

Freshly ground black
   pepper, to taste

Red pepper flakes, to
   taste

FOR THE SANDWICH

2 tablespoons olive oil

1 bell pepper of any
   color, sliced

1 cup thinly sliced red
   onion

Salt and freshly ground
   black pepper

2 cups radish greens,
   chopped

2 garlic cloves, chopped
   fine

Pinch of red pepper
   flakes

8 slices whole-grain
   bread

6 radishes, sliced into
   thin rounds

RADISHES ARE PART OF MY EARLIEST CHILDHOOD gardening memories. One winter I placed dried beans on moist paper towels in upturned jar lids and watched them sprout. I was utterly fascinated. When spring came, and it was still cold and wet, my mom suggested that I try planting radish seeds and some little onion sets outdoors in the garden. Like the beans, the radish seeds were up and growing in days. After that, I was hooked on growing vegetables.

Since radishes are cold-hardy and so easy to grow, they are in great abundance as early as March. While most people think of radishes as an ingredient to spice up a salad, my uncle considered them worthy to be the featured item in his famous radish sandwich: heavily buttered slices of fresh bread, covered with thinly sliced radishes. He would take his sandwich and a large glass of milk to the back porch swing and savor each bite. He said it was the finest meal he could imagine on a warm spring afternoon.

I've modified my uncle's recipe a bit to include radish greens sautéed in garlic, along with sweet peppers and onions. Complementing the vegetables is the creamy poppy seed spread.

To make the Poppy Seed Spread, stir all of the ingredients together in a bowl to form a smooth mixture. Set aside.

Heat the olive oil in a medium skillet over medium-high heat, and add the bell peppers and onions. Sauté until they are tender, 5 to 7 minutes. Season the peppers and onions with salt and pepper to taste, and use a slotted spoon to transfer them to a plate.

In the same skillet, stir-fry the radish greens, garlic, and red pepper flakes together over medium heat until the greens are wilted but still bright green. Just before removing the radish greens from the skillet, toss them with a pinch of salt. Add them to the plate with the peppers and onions.

Toast the bread, and then spread the Poppy Seed Spread over one side of each slice. Pile four slices with the onion mixture, and add the sliced radishes. Cover with the remaining bread slices, press down slightly, and cut in half. Serve immediately.

ROASTED CHICKEN PANINI

I REALLY LIKE THE COMBINATION of crispy exterior and warm melted gooey interior that you get in the pressed Italian sandwiches called *panini*. There are endless ways to prepare panini, but my favorite is this grilled chicken version that includes sun-dried tomatoes, tapenade, and cheese. The secret ingredient is mayonnaise, which is brushed on the outside of the sandwich before it is grilled.

While I was experimenting with ingredients, I wasn't convinced that I needed to invest in a panini press, so I created my own makeshift device using two skillets: one on the bottom to hold the sandwich and a smaller heavy skillet on top to weight the panini down. Putting a big can of stewed tomatoes in the small skillet also helped press down on the sandwich. One of these days I may get around to buying a panini press, but this works well and always gets a laugh when I put it together, so I may just stick with what I have.

SERVES 4

1 bunch fresh rosemary sprigs
2 boneless, skinless chicken breasts
4 teaspoons tapenade
4 sun-dried tomatoes packed in oil
2 garlic cloves, cut into slivers
2 tablespoons olive oil
Salt and freshly ground black pepper
1 tablespoon dried Italian seasoning (or a mixture of finely chopped fresh herbs such as oregano, basil, rosemary, and thyme)
About ⅓ cup mayonnaise
2 large crusty rolls, such as ciabatta, cut in half horizontally
½ cup grated Pecorino Romano, Parmesan, Asiago, or Grana Padano cheese

Preheat the oven to 350°F. Line an 11 x 8-inch baking dish with the rosemary sprigs, and set it aside.

Use a sharp knife to make a horizontal slit in each chicken breast, just deep enough to create a pocket. Stuff the tapenade, sun-dried tomatoes, and garlic slivers into the pockets, dividing them equally, and press pockets closed. Place the chicken breasts on top of the rosemary sprigs, and drizzle the olive oil over them. Season the chicken with a little salt and pepper, and roast for about 25 minutes, or until the chicken is cooked through. Set it aside to cool.

When the chicken is cool enough to handle, cut it into thin slices.

In a small dish, mix the Italian seasoning with ¼ cup of the mayo; spread the herbed mayo over the cut sides of the rolls. Arrange the chicken on the roll bottoms, sprinkle with the grated cheese, and add the roll tops.

Lightly spread the outside of the rolls with the remaining mayo, and then toast the sandwiches in a panini press. (Or if you are using the skillet method, weight the panini down with another heavy skillet and then set a heavy can in the top skillet.) Cook for about 3 minutes, or until the bread is toasted on the bottom. Turn the panini over, weight them down again, and toast for another 3 minutes.

Remove the panini from the press (or pan) and cut them in half. Serve immediately.

POACHED EGG AND SPINACH SALAD

I'VE ALWAYS LOVED FRESH EGGS. When I was a child, both pairs of my grandparents kept chickens, so when we would come for a visit they had plenty of eggs for meals. On my maternal side, the preferred chicken was the Silver-Laced Wyandotte. On my paternal side it was the Plymouth Rock. Both breeds are known as dual-purpose birds, meaning they are raised for their meat and as well as to produce good brown eggs. I've continued my family's poultry tradition at the Garden Home Retreat, where the chickens get the benefit of nibbling on lots of grass, insects, and table scraps, contributing to the best-tasting eggs.

Both in the garden and on the farm, I enjoy seeing the birth of new things. We use an incubator to hatch some of the eggs gathered from our chickens. My nieces and nephews come out on the weekends and enjoy seeing the chicks peck out of their eggs and emerge as wobbly-legged newborns. Then we go to the garden to see what's new since the last time they visited. Gathering spinach and a few fresh eggs along the way, they get to see firsthand where their food comes from. It's a great connection to the Earth that I enjoy sharing with them.

This salad combines the flavors of fresh eggs with spring spinach. The spinach is ready to pick just about the time the young pullets start laying their first eggs.

SERVES 6

About 1 tablespoon distilled white vinegar

4 large free-range eggs

1 pound baby spinach, rinsed thoroughly and patted dry

¾ cup extra-virgin olive oil

½ cup sherry vinegar

¼ cup balsamic vinegar

4 large shallots, thinly sliced

1 tablespoon coarsely chopped fresh thyme leaves

Salt and freshly ground black pepper

Fill a large nonstick skillet with water, and add the vinegar (to help the egg whites stay compact around the yolks). Bring the water to a boil. Then reduce the heat to a simmer (stir the water with a spoon to cool it down).

One at a time crack the eggs into a small cup or bowl, and carefully slip the eggs into the simmering water by lowering the lip of the cup ½ inch below the surface of the water and then letting the egg flow out. Use a spoon to gently nudge the egg whites closer to their yolks. Poach the eggs for approximately 4 minutes for medium-firm yolks. (Adjust the time up or down for runnier or firmer yolks, to your taste. You can test for softness/firmness by lifting an egg on a spoon and gently pressing a finger on the yolk.)

recipe continues

Using a spoon, transfer the eggs to a paper-towel-lined plate. Gently pat the top of the eggs with paper towels to remove the excess liquid.

Put the spinach in a large bowl.

Combine the olive oil, both vinegars, shallots, and thyme in a medium skillet, and boil for 1 minute.

Pour the warm dressing over the spinach, season with salt and pepper to taste, and toss. Mound the salad on plates, top each serving with a poached egg, and serve.

The best eggs for poaching are the freshest eggs you can find. Once eggs are more than a week old, the whites thin out. The whites of fresh eggs will gather compactly around the yolk, making a rounder, neater shape when poached.

SALAD OF ASPARAGUS, EDAMAME, ARUGULA, AND CHEESE

THIS SALAD CAME ABOUT as a result of my just walking through the garden to see what was ready to harvest. All the lovely spring delicacies, fresh at the same time, came together to create a salad that was as light and crisp as the season itself. Included in the ingredients is *edamame,* which is the Japanese word for fresh soybeans, harvested before they start to harden. In addition to being a great snack, shelled edamame beans are delicious served solo as a vegetable, mixed in with other vegetables, stir-fried, added to soups, or, as in this case, included in salads. In the spring, you can find edamame in farmers' markets, usually still in the pod. Because the beans are young and green when they are picked, they are soft and edible, not hard and dry like the mature soybeans that are used to make soy milk and tofu.

For this salad, their appealing sweet, nutty flavor combines nicely with the peppery taste of arugula and the crunch of blanched asparagus. The homemade version of the popular Green Goddess Dressing is the perfect topping.

SERVES 6 TO 8

8 ounces medium asparagus, trimmed

2 cups fresh edamame, or 2 cups frozen edamame, thawed

Salt and freshly ground black pepper

4 ounces arugula, coarse stems discarded, leaves rinsed thoroughly and patted dry

4 green onions, white and green parts, chopped

Green Goddess Dressing (recipe follows)

1 8-ounce piece of Pecorino Romano or Parmigiano-Reggiano cheese

Cut off the asparagus tips and set them aside. Slice the asparagus stalks lengthwise into ⅛-inch-thick slices, and set them aside. Fill a large bowl with ice and cold water, and set it aside.

Bring a large pot of salted water to a boil. Add the asparagus tips, sliced asparagus stalks, and edamame, and cook for 1 minute. Then immediately drain the vegetables in a colander and plunge them into the bowl of ice water to stop them from cooking further.

When the vegetables have cooled, drain them thoroughly and transfer them to a bowl. Add salt and pepper to taste, and toss. Divide the mixture among six to eight plates.

In a mixing bowl, toss the arugula with the green onions, and season with salt and pepper to taste. Mound equal portions of the arugula salad on top of the vegetables. Drizzle the dressing over the salads, and then use a vegetable peeler to shave thin slices of cheese on top. Serve immediately.

recipe continues

GREEN GODDESS DRESSING

MAKES 2 CUPS

SOME PEOPLE PASS ON THE ANCHOVIES, but I think they add a savory richness to this dressing.

2 cups good-quality mayonnaise (such as Hellmann's)

4 canned anchovy fillets, minced (optional)

2 tablespoons tarragon vinegar

2 green onions, white and green parts, finely chopped

2 garlic cloves, minced

¼ cup finely chopped fresh flat-leaf parsley leaves

¼ cup snipped fresh chives (¼-inch pieces)

2 tablespoons chopped fresh tarragon leaves

Salt and freshly ground black pepper

Place the mayonnaise in a small bowl, and mix in the anchovies if you like. Stir in the tarragon vinegar, green onions, garlic, parsley, chives, and tarragon, blending well. Season the dressing with salt and pepper to taste. Refrigerate leftover dressing for up to 2 weeks.

Classic French tarragon is one of the four *fines herbes* in French cooking. It imparts a delicate flavor to chicken, fish, sauces, and, of course, salad dressings. Both Texas and Mexican tarragon are good substitutes when fresh French tarragon is not readily available. All three varieties can be easily grown in container herb gardens.

SPRING LETTUCE WITH WALNUT SHERRY DRESSING

SERVES 4

FOR THE DRESSING
2 eggs, at room
    temperature
½ cup sherry vinegar
1 teaspoon sugar
1½ teaspoons minced
    garlic
½ teaspoon kosher salt
1 teaspoon cracked
    black pepper
1½ teaspoons Dijon
    mustard
½ cup walnut oil
1½ cups vegetable oil

Fresh lettuce (rinsed
    thoroughly and
    patted dry), torn
    into bite-size pieces
    (about 6 cups)
Fresh chive blossoms,
    for garnish (optional)

I LIKE SIMPLE SALADS THE BEST—particularly in the spring, when I have all kinds of lettuces growing in the garden. My favorites are among the butterhead varieties: small loose heads filled with leaves so delicate and tender they almost melt in your mouth. Lettuce is not a vegetable that is meant to give your taste buds a jolt. Its appeal is in the delicate nature of its flavor, so it's important that the dressing not overpower the lettuce.

I grow 'Butter Crunch', 'Tom Thumb', and 'Black Seeded Simpson' lettuce. Also, later in the season, I've grown 'Red Sails' and 'Red Eruption Bibb' romaine, 'Deer Tongue', 'Red Oakleaf', 'Salad Bowl', Green Oakleaf', and 'Freckles'. And I always make room for 'Rouge d'Hiver' romaine and 'White Boston' butterhead, both of which are heat-tolerant varieties.

This walnut sherry vinaigrette is one of my favorites of the house dressings at Trio's Restaurant in Little Rock. I like to throw a few chive blossoms into the salad to add sparkle. After all, chives are in full bloom when the lettuce is ready.

Bring a small pot of water to a boil. Add the eggs and cook for 1 minute. Then drain them immediately, and crack the eggs into the bowl of a food processor or blender.

Add the vinegar, sugar, garlic, salt, pepper, and Dijon mustard to the eggs, and process until smooth. With the motor running, add both oils in a slow, steady stream, processing until all of the oil is emulsified and the consistency is similar to mayonnaise. Taste, and add more salt and pepper as necessary.

Place the lettuce in a large serving bowl, and toss with ¼ to ½ cup of the dressing. Garnish with chive blossoms if you like, and serve immediately.

This recipe makes about 3 cups of Walnut Sherry Dressing. Store the extra in the refrigerator for up to 2 weeks. It is also great as a sandwich spread.

STRAWBERRY SPINACH SALAD

MIXING SPINACH AND STRAWBERRIES hadn't occurred to me until I tasted this delightful combination at a friend's house. It's one of those salads that you want to try as soon as you see it. The rich green color of the baby spinach mixed with the ruby-red strawberries is a visual delight, and the blend of flavors and textures is equally delicious: crunchy and sweet unified with a tangy dressing.

Place the spinach in a bowl and then add the strawberries, but resist the urge to mix them together.

Put all the dressing ingredients in a blender or food processor, and pulse until mixed and thickened.

Just before serving, wash your hands thoroughly and then use them to gently toss the salad with only enough dressing to coat the spinach and berries. Be careful not to bruise the spinach leaves or the berries as you mix them together. Serve immediately.

SERVES 6

1 pound fresh baby spinach, rinsed thoroughly and patted dry

2 pints fresh strawberries, hulled and halved

FOR THE DRESSING

½ cup vegetable or canola oil

¼ cup apple cider vinegar

⅓ cup sugar

1 tablespoon sesame seeds, toasted

1½ teaspoons minced onion

½ teaspoon Worcestershire sauce

1 teaspoon sea salt

½ teaspoon freshly ground black pepper

When you're ready to harvest spinach, either cut off the entire plant at the ground, or pick outer leaves that are dark green in color and about 3 to 6 inches long, and continue this every five days or so. Wash and store spinach in an airtight container in the refrigerator. It will keep for about a week.

BLACK BEAN AND SPINACH BURRITOS

SERVES 8

FOR THE BEAN MIXTURE

¼ cup vegetable or olive oil

1 onion, diced

1 green bell pepper, diced

1 teaspoon adobo seasoning (see Note), plus more to taste

2 cans black beans, drained and well rinsed

1 teaspoon ground cumin

Salt, to taste

2 cups diced fresh tomatoes

Juice of ½ lime

FOR THE REST

¼ cup olive oil

2 garlic cloves

1 pound mid-size spinach leaves, rinsed thoroughly and patted dry

8 large corn or flour tortillas, or 8 vegetable wraps

2 cups grated cheddar, Monterey Jack, or other cheese

1 cup coarsely chopped fresh cilantro leaves

THIS IS A SIMPLE AND TASTY ENTRÉE that everyone loves—especially my vegetarian friends. I always use one of my good-looking baking dishes so I can serve the burritos directly from the oven. Spinach is one of the most beautiful vegetables to grow, and it is edible from the first days of germination as micro greens.

I use whatever type of cheese I have on hand. A rich cheddar gives the burritos depth. When I'm preparing the burritos for a large group, I often use Monterey Jack inside and outside. My own preference is plain soft goat cheese on the inside and a little Jack or Manchego to sprinkle over the top.

I've also experimented with both whole wheat or corn tortillas. Although whole wheat is healthier, I prefer the taste of corn; if you let the tortillas rest between two moistened paper towels, they will be easier to work with.

Preheat the oven to 350°F. Grease a 9 x 13-inch baking dish with nonstick cooking spray and set aside.

Prepare the bean mixture: Heat the vegetable or olive oil in a medium skillet over medium-high heat, and sauté the onions, peppers, and any other veggies until they are soft and starting to turn color, about 5 minutes. Season the mixture with adobo to taste. Add the beans, toss well, and let the mixture cook down a bit with the veggies. Add the cumin, salt, and more adobo to taste. Then add the tomatoes and lime juice, and stir well. Turn the heat down and let the mixture simmer.

While the bean mixture is simmering, coat a deep frying pan with the olive oil and place it over medium heat. Crush the garlic and add it to the oil. Immediately add the spinach and toss to coat it with the oil. Cover, and allow the spinach to wilt down, about 2 to 3 minutes. You want the leaves to be soft but still be a vibrant green. Remove the spinach and the bean mixture from the heat and let cool slightly.

Place a tortilla on a plate or work surface. Near one edge of the tortilla, scatter a few pinches of grated cheese, a couple forksful of spinach, and about ½ cup of the bean mixture. Sprinkle with some cilantro. Fold the edge

recipe continues

nearest to the filling up and over the filling, just until the mixture is covered. Then fold in the two sides, envelope fashion. Roll the tortilla up to finish sealing the filling inside, and put it, seam side down, against one edge of the prepared baking dish. Continue filling, wrapping, and placing burritos in the dish until it is full. You want them touching (so they don't get too crisp), but not so close that they can't be separated later.

Sprinkle the remaining cheese in a line down the middle of the baking dish so each burrito has a strip of cheese on its midsection. Bake, uncovered, for 20 to 30 minutes (don't let them get too brown). Serve immediately.

NOTE: Adobo seasoning is a blend of garlic, oregano, and Latin spices. If you are not able to find it in the spice and seasoning section of your grocery store, you can substitute burrito seasoning, Southwest-type seasoning, or another chili-powder-based seasoning blend of your preference.

I consider spinach one of my spring elixirs, as the leaves are chock-full of vitamin A. To make sure I have plenty, I sow a few seeds every two weeks in the spring. They grow easily in raised beds or containers, as well as directly in the ground. And depending on where you live, spinach also makes a great fall crop. In the South, sowing seed in early September will yield spinach throughout the fall, winter, and early spring.

I often add one other vegetable to the bean mixture. Choose one of the following, or mix them, but if you use more than one, reduce the amount of each ingredient so the total is about 1 cup.

1 4-ounce can chopped green chiles
1 zucchini, diced
1 red bell pepper, diced
6 mushrooms, diced
Minced jalapeño pepper, to taste

GRILLED PORK CHOPS WITH ZUCCHINI AND PEPPERS

SERVES 6

FOR THE PORK CHOPS

2 tablespoons olive oil

2 tablespoons Dijon mustard

2 tablespoons balsamic or red wine vinegar

2 teaspoons fresh thyme leaves, minced

2 garlic cloves, minced

¼ teaspoon salt

¼ teaspoon freshly ground black pepper

6 pork chops, about 1 inch thick

FOR THE VEGETABLES

1 red bell pepper, sliced top to bottom into 6 pieces

3 small zucchini, sliced in half lengthwise

1 medium sweet onion, sliced top to bottom into 6 pieces

1 tablespoon olive oil

½ teaspoon salt

½ teaspoon freshly ground black pepper

Fresh thyme sprigs, for garnish

AS ANYONE WHO HAS GROWN just one zucchini plant can tell you, this squash is undoubtedly one of the most abundant producers in the entire plant kingdom. Just one plant yields so many green sausage-shaped vegetables that one can hardly find enough uses for it all. This is a fast and delicious way to use several zucchini in one dish. When they are grilled with a medley of other summer vegetables and served with some well-seasoned grilled pork chops, you have a simple meal without spending all day in the kitchen and having a lot to clean up.

I like to put the chops and the marinade in a zip-top plastic bag in the morning and leave them in the fridge until it's time to grill later that evening. When grilling pork chops, I try to undercook the meat just slightly because the chops tend to keep cooking after I take them off the grill.

Fresh thyme is handy to have around to snip and sprinkle on the meat and vegetables before they come off the grill. Try growing thyme in containers. It is one of the easiest herbs to grow, and in a dish like this, the added fresh flavor is excellent.

In a small bowl, combine the 2 tablespoons olive oil with the mustard, vinegar, thyme, garlic, salt, and pepper. Set aside 2 tablespoons of the mustard mixture in the fridge. Spread the remaining mixture over both sides of the chops. Place the chops in a zip-top plastic bag and leave them in the fridge to marinate for 4 to 8 hours.

Preheat an outdoor grill to medium-high heat.

Grill the pork chops 4 to 6 inches from the heat for 5 to 6 minutes on each side, or until a meat thermometer reads 160°F.

Toss the bell peppers, zucchini, and onions into a large iron skillet. Drizzle the olive oil over the vegetables, and sprinkle with the salt and pepper. While the chops are grilling, sauté the vegetable mixture on the grill until the veggies are crisp-tender. Stir in the reserved mustard mixture, and toss to coat the vegetables. Strip the tiny leaves from several fresh sprigs of thyme and sprinkle them on the meat and vegetables before they come off the grill.

Serve the vegetables with the pork chops.

CRAWFISH (OR SHRIMP) ÉTOUFFÉE

WHEN YOU HAVE BEEN FRIENDS with someone for over thirty-five years and most of that time has been centered around delicious food, you develop a respect for each other's opinions and tastes. This describes my friendship with Teri Bunce, a gifted cook who has prepared many meals at the Garden Home Retreat.

Teri has elevated the crawfish boil to haute cuisine with this dish. Out-of-town visitors are reluctant to try crawfish, but after dining on this presentation they often ask for the recipe. A crawfish has five pairs of swimmerets under its abdomen, which helps it navigate backward. So if someone says to you, "Don't start crawfishing on me," they mean don't start backing up on what you said.

Crawfish are readily available in the southeast from early spring until around Mother's Day. Shrimp is equally delicious.

Thoroughly combine the salt, cayenne pepper, white and black peppers, dried basil, and dried thyme in a small bowl, and set aside. (If you are using fresh basil and thyme, do not add them here; hold them until you add the green onions in the last step so that the fresh herbs won't scorch.)

In a separate bowl, combine the onions, celery, and bell peppers. Heat the oil in a large cast-iron Dutch oven over high heat until it begins to smoke, 5 to 6 minutes. Using a long-handled metal whisk, gradually mix in the flour, whisking until smooth. Continue cooking, whisking constantly, until the roux is dark red-brown, the color of an old penny. Be careful not to let it scorch in the pan or splash on your skin.

Remove the pan from the heat and immediately stir in the onion mixture with a wooden spoon. Stir in the reserved seasoning mix and continue stirring until the mixture has cooled, about 5 minutes.

Return the pan to medium heat. Gradually add 2 cups of the stock to the roux and whisk until the roux is thoroughly dissolved. Reduce heat to low and cook, whisking almost constantly, until the flour taste is gone, about 2 minutes. Add the butter, green onions, remaining 1 cup stock, and the crawfish. (If you are using fresh basil and thyme, add those ingredients now.) Cook until the crawfish turn pink and tender and are cooked through, about 10 minutes.

Ladle the étouffée over hot rice in soup bowls, and serve.

SERVES 8

2 teaspoons salt

1 teaspoon cayenne pepper

1 teaspoon ground white pepper

1 teaspoon freshly ground black pepper

1 teaspoon dried basil, or 1 tablespoon finely chopped fresh sweet basil leaves

½ teaspoon dried thyme leaves, or 1½ teaspoons finely minced fresh thyme leaves

¼ cup chopped onions

¼ cup chopped celery

¼ cup chopped green bell peppers

7 tablespoons vegetable oil

¾ cup all-purpose flour

3 cups seafood stock or bottled clam juice

12 tablespoons (1½ sticks) butter, at room temperature, cut into pieces

1 cup finely chopped green onions, white and green parts

2 pounds medium crawfish tails, or 2 pounds shrimp, peeled and deveined

4 cups hot cooked white rice

GRILLADES AND CREAMY GRITS

SERVES 6 TO 8

GRILLADES

4 pounds boneless round steak, ½ inch thick

1 cup all-purpose flour

½ cup bacon drippings or vegetable oil

1 cup chopped onions

2 cups chopped green onions, white and green parts

1 cup chopped green bell peppers

¾ cup chopped celery

2 garlic cloves, minced

2 cups peeled, seeded, and chopped tomatoes

2 cups water

2 cups red wine

3 teaspoons salt

½ teaspoon freshly ground black pepper

2 bay leaves

½ teaspoon Tabasco sauce

2 tablespoons Worcestershire sauce

3 tablespoons chopped fresh parsley leaves

CREAMY GRITS

1¼ cups quick-cooking grits

2 cups milk

1½ cups chicken broth

½ cup heavy cream

THE CHATELAINE OF RAVENNA, a beautiful 1830s Greek Revival house in Natchez, Mississippi, shared this recipe for grillades (pronounced *gree*-yahds) with me. It is one she brought up from her people in New Orleans. While there are many versions of the story about the origins of this dish, it is believed that it started as part of the traditional country hog butchering (also known as *boucherie*), when thinly sliced pieces of fresh pork were pan-fried with sliced onions or skewered on sticks. The cooking took place in black iron pots over the *boucherie* fires. The grillades were then eaten over grits or rice throughout the day.

Today, grillades and grits is a traditional Louisiana Sunday brunch dish—often called the Cajun answer to the Low Country's shrimp and grits. While the meat in the original recipe was pork, others call for lightly pounded veal or top round steak. I prefer the round steak, and I cut it into strips as you would for beef stroganoff. I serve them over grits cooked with milk and whipping cream. One of the things I find most interesting about grillades is that it is one of those dishes that has a place on all rungs of the social ladder.

Remove the fat from the meat, and pound it to ¼-inch thickness. Cut the meat into pieces about ½ inch wide and several inches long.

Place ½ cup of the flour in a bowl, add the beef strips, and toss to coat them with the flour.

Heat ¼ cup of the bacon drippings in a Dutch oven over medium-high heat. Shaking off any excess flour, add the beef strips and cook, stirring frequently, until they are browned, 5 to 7 minutes. Using a slotted spoon, transfer the meat to a plate and set it aside.

Add the remaining ¼ cup bacon drippings to the Dutch oven and stir in the remaining ½ cup flour. Cook, stirring, over medium-high heat until you have a dark brown roux, 4 to 5 minutes. Then add both types of onions and the green peppers, celery, and garlic. Sauté until soft, about 5 to 6 minutes.

Return the meat to the Dutch oven; add the tomatoes, water, and wine (the mixture should cover the meat), and stir well. Cook for a few minutes. Then add the salt, pepper, bay leaves, Tabasco, Worcestershire, and parsley.

Bring to a boil. Reduce the heat to a simmer and cook slowly, stirring occasionally, for about 2 hours or until the meat is very tender. Let the grillades sit for several hours or refrigerate overnight. Rewarm in a Dutch oven over medium heat.

Combine the grits, milk, and broth in a medium saucepan, and bring to a boil over medium-high heat. Reduce the heat to low and simmer, stirring occasionally, for 4 to 5 minutes or until thickened. Remove from the heat, and stir in the cream.

Spoon the grits onto serving plates, top with the grillades, and serve.

ARUGULA
PESTO ON . . .

MAKES 1 CUP

3 garlic cloves

½ cup chopped
   walnuts, toasted

3 cups (packed) fresh
   arugula leaves, rinsed
   thoroughly and
   patted dry

½ cup fresh flat-leaf
   parsley leaves

2 tablespoons fresh
   lemon juice

⅓ cup olive oil, plus
   extra for covering the
   surface

⅓ cup freshly grated
   Parmesan cheese

½ teaspoon salt

¼ teaspoon freshly
   ground black pepper

I'll admit it, I'm nuts over arugula. Known as the king of gourmet salad greens, arugula's dark green leaves have a sharp, peppery taste and form an open head. Even if all you have is an eight-inch pot on your back porch, you can grow it. All you need is an area that gets at least six hours of sun. (It will grow in less, but the leaves won't be quite as flavorful.)

This pesto recipe lets me enjoy arugula in a variety of ways. After I make up a batch I find all kinds of things to combine it with, from potatoes to pasta, tomatoes to shrimp. It really is that tasty and versatile.

Begin by dropping the garlic cloves into a food processor fitted with the metal blade. Whirl the garlic around for a few seconds to chop it up (this will save you from having to do it by hand). Add the toasted walnuts, arugula, parsley, and lemon juice, and process until all the ingredients are finely chopped.

With the motor running, drizzle the ⅓ cup olive oil into the processor; process until the mixture is blended and smooth.

Turn the food processor off and add the Parmesan cheese, salt, and pepper. You may need to scrape down the sides of the bowl at this point. Pulse several times until all the ingredients are well incorporated.

Transfer the pesto to a container, and using the back of a spoon, smooth it until it is level. Pour a thin layer of olive oil over the top (to keep the arugula from turning an off color). To get to the pesto beneath the olive oil, simply tilt the container slightly to one side. The pesto will keep, covered, in the refrigerator for about 5 days.

Now, what to mix it with? Here are a few ideas:

- Toss the pesto with cooked pasta of your choice and mix in some oil-packed sun-dried tomatoes.
- Cook up some farfalle pasta, and toss it with some of the pesto and a little of the pasta water to thin it out a bit. Add a pinch of red pepper flakes and some halved cherry tomatoes, and garnish with shaved Parmesan cheese.

- Mix the pesto with grilled shrimp or scallops.
- Microwave new potatoes until they are fork-tender. Then coarsely chop them and mix them with the pesto.
- Butter two slices of good bread. Spread the pesto on the unbuttered side of one slice, and then top with grated Gruyère (or a cheese of your choice). Add the other slice of bread, unbuttered side down. Toast the sandwich in a skillet until it is golden brown on both sides and the cheese is melted and gooey. Serve with tomato soup or a salad.

Arugula seeds should be sown directly in the ground when temperatures are cool. In my mid-South garden I grow arugula in the spring and fall. If you live in an area where summers are mild, you can grow arugula continuously over the season by sowing seeds every week or two.

If you want to grow arugula in a raised bed or an in-ground garden, sprinkle the seeds in narrow furrows that are 5 inches apart, and cover them with ¼ to ½ inch of soil. Keep the soil evenly moist, and the seeds will germinate in about 10 days. The plants are ready to harvest in about 5 weeks. For the best flavor, harvest the leaves when they are 3 to 4 inches tall and just beginning to form lobes. If the leaves become too mature, they can taste bitter.

RADISH TOP PASTA

IF YOU HAVE NEVER GARDENED but want to give it a try, you should start with radishes. They will help you get over any fear you may have about planting seeds directly in the ground. And they will produce more bounty in the shortest period of time of any vegetable I can think of. My 'Easter Egg' radishes were planted on February 15 and I harvested a big bunch for this salad twenty-eight days later. Now let's face it, most people would not consider a radish a very sexy vegetable, but I adore them. If you live with a prejudice about radishes, you clearly haven't explored the range of varieties, flavors, and creative ways of using them. After all, Scarlett O'Hara appreciated radishes. She held one to the sky after Union forces burned her beloved Tara (during the War of Northern Aggression) and swore she'd find a way out of that big mess.

For this recipe, slice the radishes thin so they are almost translucent. The shape, color, and flavor of these red globes make them the perfect complement to penne pasta. And don't throw away those bright green leafy tops—they add a tangy spark to this dish.

SERVES 6

About 25 radishes, with leaves

12 ounces small pasta, such as penne

½ cup pine nuts

3 tablespoons extra-virgin olive oil

1 onion, chopped

1 garlic clove, finely chopped

Salt and freshly ground black pepper

⅓ cup freshly grated Parmesan cheese, plus more for serving

½ cup chopped fresh parsley leaves

Wash and dry the radishes and the green tops. Cut the leaves from the radishes and set them aside. Cut off the top and bottom of each radish, then slice them paper-thin. Next, chop the radish leaves.

Fill a large saucepan with salted water and bring it to a boil. Add the pasta and cook it according to the package instructions.

While the pasta is cooking, toast the pine nuts in a dry skillet over medium-high heat until lightly browned, about 4 minutes. Set the nuts aside.

Heat the olive oil in the same skillet over medium-high heat. Add the onions and cook until they become translucent, 4 to 6 minutes. Add the sliced radishes and cook for 2 minutes longer. Add the garlic, toasted pine nuts, and radish leaves, and cook until the leaves wilt and soften. Remove the pan from the heat, season the mixture with salt and pepper to taste, and keep warm.

Drain the pasta, leaving a couple of tablespoons of water in the pan. Add the radish mixture and the Parmesan, and mix. Serve topped with the chopped parsley. Pass more Parmesan at the table.

GINGER-SESAME STIR-FRIED ASPARAGUS

SERVES 6

1½ pounds asparagus, trimmed and cut into 2-inch pieces

2 tablespoons olive oil

½ large red bell pepper, cut into strips

1 tablespoon chopped fresh ginger

1 tablespoon soy sauce

¼ teaspoon red pepper flakes, or to taste

2 teaspoons toasted sesame oil

1 teaspoon sesame seeds

THIS IS ONE OF MY FAVORITE SIDE DISHES for both spring and summer—the combination makes for a dynamic visual presentation. In spring, when my asparagus is plentiful, all I have to do is pick up a red bell pepper at the market. Likewise in summer, after the garden asparagus has "done its thing," we have loads of red bell peppers, and I can find asparagus at the store. When preparing this dish, be careful not to overcook the asparagus. It's best when it is slightly al dente or crunchy—not limp and overdone. The Asian seasoning gives the dish a nice spark.

I grow three varieties of asparagus in my garden: 'Purple Passion', which is a beautiful purple-stemmed variety, UC157 (not a sexy name, but a real producer), and 'Atlas', also an excellent newer hybrid. In my opinion, these varieties are superior to older standards such as 'Mary Washington' and 'Jersey Giant' because they have higher yields, can withstand warmer temperatures, and exhibit better disease resistance.

Available year-round thanks to shipments from the Southern Hemisphere, asparagus is in its peak season in the United States from late February through July. When shopping, select crisp, tightly closed, straight spears with fresh-looking cut ends. Avoid those that are limp or show signs of drying at the end.

Bring ¼ inch of water to a boil in a large nonstick skillet over high heat. Add the asparagus pieces and return to a boil. Then reduce the heat to low, cover the skillet, and simmer for 5 minutes, or until crisp-tender.

Drain the asparagus in a colander and run it briefly under cold running water to stop the cooking. Drain it again. Wipe the skillet dry with a paper towel.

Heat the olive oil in the same skillet over high heat. Add the bell peppers and cook, stirring constantly, for about 3 minutes, or until just tender. Add the asparagus, ginger, soy sauce, and red pepper flakes, and cook for 2 minutes or until heated through. Remove the skillet from the heat and stir in the sesame oil and sesame seeds.

Turn out onto a platter, and serve warm.

BROCCOLI WITH LEMON AND HAZELNUTS

SERVES 6

4 cups broccoli florets

½ cup hazelnuts, roughly chopped

Grated zest and juice of 2 lemons

6 tablespoons hazelnut oil

½ teaspoon sea salt

¼ teaspoon ground white pepper

AS A MEMBER IN GOOD STANDING of the mustard and cabbage family, broccoli has a mild mustard taste that pairs well with several kinds of nuts, such as almonds, pine nuts, and, as in the case of this recipe, hazelnuts. Make this ahead of time and serve chilled from the fridge, as you would a salad.

This is an easy and delicious way to prepare broccoli, especially for those who might otherwise turn up their noses at this wonderful vegetable. I've had great success serving it to my nieces and nephews, who have even asked for second helpings. Imagine that!

Fill a large bowl with ice and cold water, and set it aside.

Bring water to a simmer in the bottom of a vegetable steamer. Add the broccoli to the steamer basket, cover the pan, and steam until the florets are al dente—tender but still with some firmness—about 5 to 7 minutes.

Plunge the broccoli into the ice water to stop the cooking and retain its vibrant green color. When it has cooled thoroughly, drain it well and set it aside in a large bowl.

Toast the chopped hazelnuts in a nonstick skillet over medium heat until they are lightly golden. Be sure to keep the nuts moving in the pan so they do not burn. Set the nuts aside to cool.

Whisk the lemon zest, juice, hazelnut oil, sea salt, and white pepper together in a small bowl. Pour most of the mixture over the broccoli, and toss it all together to make sure the broccoli is well coated with the vinaigrette (I like to use my fingers for this). Sprinkle in the toasted hazelnuts, and then arrange the broccoli on a serving platter. Spoon a little more vinaigrette over the top, and serve.

Most people are afraid to plant broccoli early. Not me. One of broccoli's best attributes is its ability to grow in cool weather. That means it is one of the earliest vegetables I can grow in the spring, when I'm so hungry for something fresh from the garden. I can also enjoy it in the fall as summer temperatures begin to cool. One trick I've learned is to drop a few broccoli seeds among the seedling plants. That helps keep an ever-ripening succession of broccoli going strong. The varieties I like are 'Green Comet', 'Packman', and 'Premium Crop'.

BUTTERED SPRING PEAS WITH CHOPPED MINT

SERVES 6

Milk or water

About 6 leaves green
loose-leaf lettuce,
rinsed thoroughly
and patted dry

4 cups shelled fresh
English peas

4 tablespoons (½ stick)
butter

Juice of ½ lemon

3 or 4 fresh mint leaves,
minced

Salt and freshly ground
black pepper

WHEN A VEGETABLE IS AS WONDERFUL AS FRESH PEAS, it needs little embellishment. This simple recipe is a combination of one my grandmother gave me and one Regina Charboneau shared with me when she was the chef at Monmouth Plantation in Natchez, Mississippi.

Peas are members of the legume family, the third-largest family among the flowering plants. As a food group, legumes were so highly regarded in ancient Rome that the names of prominent Roman families were used in naming them: Fabius for the faba or fava bean, Lentulus for the lentil, Cicero for the chickpea, and Piso for the pea. And so it goes (or, and so it went)?

Pour milk into a medium saucepan to a depth of about ¼ inch. Line the bottom of the pan with a layer of lettuce leaves (it is okay if the leaves overlap). Add the peas and 1 tablespoon of the butter. Cover the peas and butter with a second layer of lettuce leaves.

Cook over low heat until the liquid begins to bubble. Then continue cooking for another 5 to 10 minutes, until the peas are crisp-tender.

While the peas are cooking, melt the remaining 3 tablespoons butter in a separate saucepan over low heat. Add the lemon juice.

Drain the peas, discarding the lettuce leaves. Add the peas, mint, and salt and pepper to taste to the lemon butter, and stir to mix. Spoon into a serving bowl, and serve.

SPRING ONION AND HERB RISOTTO

WANT TO SAVE SOME MONEY and enjoy your food even more? Grow herbs! Starting a kitchen herb garden is a great way to have your favorite seasonings on hand for a fraction of what they cost at the market. Herbs are easy to grow and will happily produce healthy plants in small pots on your windowsill, balcony, or patio. It's fun to step out the door with scissors in hand and snip a few fresh leaves to add to your meals.

This recipe takes advantage of all those wonderful spring herbs that are bursting with flavor in the early months of the growing season. I'll leave the blend up to you. My favorite is equal parts of basil, chives, and flat-leaf parsley, but one of my friends prepares this risotto with mint, parsley, and rosemary. If you are growing onions, once the sets take hold and begin to grow, you can begin harvesting a few young ones to add to dishes such as this risotto.

Bring the chicken broth to a simmer in a saucepan, and keep it at a bare simmer.

Heat the olive oil in a large heavy-bottomed skillet over low heat, and sauté the green onions and celery until translucent, about 5 to 6 minutes. Be careful not to allow them to brown. Add the rice and stir it to coat with the olive oil. Sauté the rice with the onions and celery for about 6 minutes.

Add the wine and cook, stirring, for 1 minute. Then stir in ½ cup of the simmering broth and cook over moderate heat, stirring constantly and keeping at a strong simmer throughout, until the broth has been absorbed. Continue cooking at a stronger simmer, adding the broth about ½ cup at a time and stirring constantly until each addition has been absorbed before adding the next, until the rice is tender and creamy-looking but still al dente, 18 to 20 minutes total. There may be some broth left over.

Stir in the herbs, cheese, and salt and pepper to taste, and serve the risotto immediately.

SERVES 6

1½ quarts chicken broth

3 tablespoons olive oil

¼ cup finely chopped green onions, white and green parts

1 large celery rib, finely chopped

1½ cups Arborio rice

½ cup dry white wine

1½ cups finely chopped mixed fresh herbs, such as parsley, basil, oregano, and chives

⅓ cup freshly grated Parmigiano-Reggiano cheese

Salt and freshly ground black pepper

NEW POTATOES WITH PARSLEY

SERVES 6

10 to 12 new potatoes
(about 1½ pounds)

2 tablespoons butter,
melted

2 tablespoons chopped
fresh parsley leaves

Salt and freshly ground
black pepper, to taste

A POPULAR TREND IN COOKING is harvesting young or immature vegetables, such as baby peas or immature corn on the cob or micro greens. But ever since people have been planting potatoes, they have been digging them up before they are fully developed and calling them "new" potatoes, or sometimes "creamers" or "fingerlings." New potatoes are not a separate variety of potato, but just young versions of various types of potatoes.

This is a practice I completely understand, as I would call myself an impatient gardener. It's hard to wait until potatoes are fully mature, which is usually midsummer. So once the potato plants begin to flower, I can dig into the side of a mound of them and pull out a few little ones. In their young form, the skin of new potatoes is generally thinner than the skin found on older potatoes, so they are tender and delicious. Because new potatoes are very small, they are also well suited to boiling and roasting.

In the market, look for new potatoes sold individually or by the bag. Buying individual potatoes for a single meal can guarantee less waste but is generally more expensive than buying them by the bag.

This recipe is easy to prepare and celebrates the first potato harvest.

Pour water into a Dutch oven to a depth of 1 inch. Cover, and bring to a boil over high heat.

In the meantime, wash the potatoes and remove a strip of skin around the "equator" of each potato, if desired.

Add the potatoes to the boiling water, cover, and return to a boil. Then reduce the heat and cook for 20 to 25 minutes, or until tender. Drain, and return the potatoes to the Dutch oven.

Drizzle the melted butter over the potatoes; then sprinkle with the parsley, salt, and pepper. Stir gently to coat the potatoes, and serve.

MOM'S CINNAMON ROLLS

I'D NEVER HEAR THE END OF IT if I didn't include this recipe. Every Christmas morning, my family would get up at the crack of dawn, tear through the presents, and then gobble up my Mom's homemade cinnamon rolls. These rolls just taste like home.

Prepare the dough: Combine the milk, sugar, salt, and 3 tablespoons of butter in a saucepan; heat until the butter melts. Let cool to 105° to 115°F.

Dissolve the yeast in the warm water in a large mixing bowl; let it stand for 5 minutes. Stir in the milk mixture, 1½ cups flour, and the egg; beat with an electric mixer at medium speed until smooth. Stir in ¾ cup flour.

Turn the dough out onto a lightly floured surface, and knead it until it is smooth and elastic, about 8 minutes. Place it in a well-buttered bowl, and turn it around to grease the top. Cover with a clean dishcloth, and let the dough rise in a warm (85°F), draft-free place for 1 hour (the dough will not quite double in bulk).

Butter an 8-inch square baking dish, and set it aside.

Punch the dough down and then turn it out onto a lightly floured surface. Roll the dough into a 12 x 8-inch rectangle. Combine 4 tablespoons softened butter, brown sugar, and cinnamon in a small bowl, and mix well. Spread the filling evenly over the dough. Starting at a long side, roll the dough up jelly-roll fashion to form a tight cylinder. Pinch the seam to seal (do not seal the ends). Cut the roll into twelve 1-inch-thick slices. Place the slices, cut side down, in the baking dish. Brush the tops with the melted butter. Using a fork, gently lift the center of the rolls to form a peak.

Cover the pan with a clean dishcloth and let the dough rise in a warm, draft-free place for about 40 minutes (the rolls will not double in bulk).

Preheat the oven to 350°F. Bake the rolls for 35 minutes.

In a small bowl, combine the powdered sugar, cream cheese, and milk, stirring well; spread the icing over the warm rolls. Gently remove the warm rolls to a serving platter.

MAKES 12 ROLLS

FOR THE ROLLS
¼ cup milk
¼ cup sugar
½ teaspoon salt
3 tablespoons butter
1 envelope active dry yeast
¼ cup warm water (105° to 115°F)
2¼ cups all-purpose flour
1 egg, at room temperature
4 tablespoons (½ stick) butter, at room temperature
½ cup firmly packed light brown sugar
1 teaspoon ground cinnamon
1 tablespoon butter, melted

FOR THE ICING
1½ cups sifted powdered sugar
2 tablespoons cream cheese, at room temperature
2 tablespoons milk

PINEAPPLE-ORANGE FRENCH TOAST

I LOOK FOR ANY EXCUSE TO USE MY FRESH EGGS, and this French toast recipe is one of the best. I like to really soak generous slices of bread to take up plenty of the egg, but if you prefer your French toast not so moist, dip the bread slices in the egg batter just long enough to coat each side. As a child, I loved French toast. My mother would make it to enjoy as a special weekend treat or as a birthday breakfast. Real maple syrup is my choice for topping, but these are just as tasty with a dusting of powdered sugar (that's how Mom topped them). I also enjoy this recipe during peach season: I add sliced fresh peaches on top, and then pour the peach juice over the French toast.

Preheat the oven to 325°F.

Melt the butter in a 10 x 15-inch jelly-roll pan. Combine the sugar, cinnamon, and orange zest in a small bowl, and sprinkle the mixture over the melted butter.

In a separate bowl, stir the eggs and juice together. Dip the bread slices in the egg mixture, soaking them well, and then arrange them on top of the butter-sugar mixture.

Bake for 20 minutes, until lightly browned. Lift out the slices and invert them onto serving plates. Serve with butter and your favorite syrup.

SERVES 4

4 tablespoons (½ stick) butter

⅓ cup sugar

¼ teaspoon ground cinnamon

1 teaspoon grated orange zest

4 eggs, lightly beaten

⅔ cup pineapple-orange juice

8 thick slices firm white bread, or 1 long loaf French bread, cut into 1-inch-thick slices

Butter, for serving, at room temperature

Maple or other syrup, for serving, warmed

ALL-AMERICAN BLUEBERRY MUFFINS

MAKES 12 MUFFINS

6 tablespoons (¾ stick) butter, at room temperature

¾ cup plus 2 teaspoons sugar

1 egg

2 cups all-purpose flour

½ teaspoon salt

2 teaspoons baking powder

½ cup milk

1 teaspoon vanilla extract

1 pint fresh blueberries

1 teaspoon ground cinnamon

AS KIDS, MY SIBLINGS AND I spent many a summer day roaming the woods searching for huckleberries. That's what we called the wild blueberries that grew on large bushes at the edge of the woods, where the trees met the pasture. My Aunt Genny used to tell us how my great-grandmother and other relatives would go picking, shaking the huckleberry bushes to harvest the berries. They would take buckets and a large bed sheet, lay the sheet at the base of the huckleberry bush, and shake the branches. The ripe berries would fall, and they would pick up the corners of the sheet and pour them into the buckets. In my day, most of the fruit was made into preserves, but we also enjoyed them in muffins. I like this family recipe because it has plenty of blueberries and the muffins aren't too sweet, which makes them great with mimosas.

Preheat the oven to 375°F. Butter a standard 12-cup muffin tin.

In a large mixing bowl, cream the butter with the ¾ cup sugar, using an electric beater. Add the egg and beat until it is well incorporated.

In a separate bowl, combine the flour, salt, and baking powder. Fold half the dry ingredients into the butter mixture. Stir in ¼ cup of the milk. Then repeat the process with the remaining dry ingredients and milk.

Add the vanilla and give the batter a good stir. Now gently fold the blueberries into the batter. Spoon the batter into the muffin cups, filling them almost level to the top. Mix the remaining 2 teaspoons sugar with the cinnamon, and sprinkle the cinnamon-sugar on top of the muffin batter. Bake for 30 minutes.

If you can stand to wait, remove the muffins from the tin and let cool on a wire rack. Otherwise, get 'em while they're hot!

BANANA DELIGHT

MY GREAT-GRANDMOTHER'S PARENTS had an enormous pecan grove at their place in Lonoke County, Arkansas. In the fall there was always a plentitude of nuts littering the grounds, and we kids gathered them up like mad squirrels.

While I don't grow my own pecans at the Garden Home Retreat, I do maintain a steady appetite for this dessert. It is one of my favorite ways to end a good meal at Trio's Restaurant in Little Rock. It is smooth, sweet, and creamy on the inside, with a great crust and topped with a sprinkling of toasted coconut. I think it's the crust that keeps me coming back for more; it is a special blend of shortbread and pecans that creates a delightful contrast of textures and flavors to what is otherwise a dolled-up version of banana pudding. And there's no getting around it: I have a weakness for just about anything with pecans.

Preheat the oven to 350°F.

Make the crust: In a medium mixing bowl, blend together the flour, butter, and pecans. Pat the mixture evenly over the bottom of a 9 x 13-inch baking pan, and bake for 25 minutes. Remove the pan from the oven and let the crust cool completely before continuing with the next layers.

Make the cream cheese filling: Using an electric mixer, beat the cream cheese and heavy cream together in a medium mixing bowl. Add the powdered sugar and continue to beat until the filling is smooth and thick. Spread the mixture evenly over the cooled crust.

Next, make the pudding layer: In a medium mixing bowl, whisk the milk with the pudding mix until it is thickened. Spread it carefully over the cream cheese layer. (You can prepare the dessert to this point a day ahead. Cover and refrigerate.) Cover the pudding layer with the sliced bananas.

For the topping, use an electric mixer to beat the heavy cream in a small bowl until it is fluffy and spreadable; add the confectioners' sugar. Gently spread it over the banana layer, pushing the whipped cream to the edges of the pan, covering the bananas well. Sprinkle the top with the toasted pecans and toasted coconut. Cover and refrigerate for 1 hour.

To serve, cut into portions and put on dessert plates.

SERVES 10

FOR THE CRUST

2 cups all-purpose flour

1 cup (2 sticks) butter, melted and cooled

1 cup chopped pecans

FOR THE CREAM CHEESE FILLING

8 ounces cream cheese, at room temperature

1 cup heavy cream

1 cup sifted powdered sugar

FOR THE PUDDING AND BANANAS

2 cups cold whole milk

1 cup instant vanilla pudding mix

2 to 3 ripe bananas, thinly sliced

FOR THE TOPPING

2 cups heavy cream

½ cup confectioners' sugar

½ cup chopped pecans, toasted

½ cup sweetened flaked coconut, toasted

SPECKLED
STRAWBERRY
ICE CREAM

SERVES 6 TO 8

1 quart fresh
    strawberries
Juice of 1 orange
1 cup heavy cream
¾ cup superfine sugar
2 teaspoons freshly
    ground black pepper,
    or to taste

AT THE GARDEN HOME RETREAT we have a twenty-foot round bed under the old Brown Turkey fig tree, affectionately called "Miss Big Fig." The entire bed at her feet is planted with 'Cardinal' strawberries. They make a great ground cover under the spreading limbs of the fig tree (we like to say that the strawberry plants help to cover the ol' girl's ankles), and children especially love to pick the berries as they ripen. One of my favorite strawberry treats is to make ice cream from the just-picked fruit.

This combination of strawberries and black pepper is a truly delicious blend of flavors. Strawberries have such an interesting history: during the Middle Ages, they represented purity and innocence. Black pepper likewise has its own fascinating history: at one time it was so highly prized that it was used as currency. Blending the two in this recipe combines sweetness with mystery. Once you taste it, I think you'll agree.

Hull the strawberries, and combine them with the orange juice in a food processor. Process to form a puree. Then add the cream and sugar, and process until well mixed.

Next, season the mixture with the pepper. If you are tasting the blend as you mix, keep in mind that the flavor will be milder when frozen than it is now at room temperature. Pulse the processor a few more times to mix the pepper in.

Pour the mixture into an ice cream maker and freeze according to the manufacturer's directions. Serve immediately, or pack in plastic containers for the freezer.

If you don't have an ice cream maker, place the mixture in a shallow container and freeze until it is half frozen. Then put the mixture back into the food processor and pulse until it is smooth. Return it to the freezer to freeze completely.

Transfer the ice cream from the freezer to the fridge 30 minutes before serving so it softens slightly.

CHEF LEE'S FLAN WITH ALLEN'S FLOWERS

I HAVE A LARGE FLOCK OF LAYING HENS, and most of the eggs they produce go to a well-known local restaurant, Ashley's, at the Capital Hotel. The culinary team at Ashley's came to the Garden Home Retreat to see the farm and tour the gardens, and brought along this dessert they had created with my eggs. I loved it. This traditional Mexican dessert is as light as a cloud.

I keep citrus of all kinds in various containers around the greenhouse, so it's easy to pick off a few blossoms for an intoxicating garnish. The fresh orange slices and fragrant blossoms make this dish a feast for all the senses.

SERVES 8 TO 10

⅔ cup sugar
¼ cup water
1 tablespoon light corn syrup
1 14-ounce can sweetened condensed milk
½ cup half-and-half
1 cup whole milk
1 3-inch cinnamon stick
5 large eggs, at room temperature
¾ teaspoon vanilla extract
1 orange, segmented
Orange or other fresh flowers, for garnish (optional)
Sweetened whipped cream, for serving

Combine the sugar, water, and corn syrup in a small, heavy saucepan, and bring to a boil over medium-high heat. Continue to cook, swirling the pan rather than stirring the mixture, until the syrup is a deep amber color, 7 to 10 minutes. Immediately pour the caramel into a ceramic or glass pie dish. Tilt the dish to distribute it evenly over the bottom and a little up the sides. Set the dish aside.

Preheat the oven to 325°F. Bring a saucepan or tea kettle of water to a boil.

Combine the condensed milk, half-and-half, whole milk, and cinnamon stick in a large saucepan, and bring to a simmer over medium heat. Remove from the heat. Discard the cinnamon stick. In a bowl, lightly whisk the eggs until blended. Gradually whisk the eggs into the warm milk mixture, and then whisk in the vanilla.

Place the prepared pie dish in a large roasting pan, and strain the custard mixture through a fine-mesh sieve into the pie dish. Place the roasting pan on the center rack of the oven. Then pour boiling water into the roasting pan to a depth of 1 inch, surrounding the pie dish.

Bake, uncovered, until the flan is just set but still has a light jiggle to it, 1 to 1½ hours. A knife inserted in the middle should come out clean.

recipe continues

Remove the pie dish from the oven and place it on a wire rack to cool. Once it has cooled completely, wrap the top of the dish with plastic wrap and refrigerate it for at least 6 hours or for up to 2 days.

To unmold the flan, run a knife around the inside edge of the pie dish. Invert a rimmed serving plate over the dish and invert the plate and flan together. Lift off the pie dish carefully. If the flan has not released, run a knife along the edge of the flan and try to help it out gently.

Decorate the edge of the flan with orange segments and a few flower blossoms, if using, and a dollop of lightly sweetened whipped cream. When ready to serve, cut the flan into wedges and add a touch of the whipped cream.

RASPBERRY CHEESE TART

FRESH RASPBERRIES ARE FRAGRANTLY SWEET and have a near "melt-in-your-mouth" texture. They are so easy to grow. Actually, the hardest part of growing them is getting them from the bush to the kitchen. Most of them disappear en route!

Raspberry plants are either summer-fruiting or ever-bearing. If you have summer-fruiting raspberries, they will produce fruit on canes that grew the previous year. The ever-bearers will produce fruit on last year's canes and also on new canes. The most common kind of raspberry is red-pink in color, but others come in black, purple, orange, yellow, and white. All are delicious.

I love to eat them any way they are fixed—blended in beverages, added to salads, or in desserts such as this delightful cheese tart.

SERVES 8 TO 10

FOR THE CRUST

8 tablespoons (1 stick) unsalted butter, at room temperature

¼ cup light brown sugar, packed

1 large egg, at room temperature, lightly beaten

1½ cups all-purpose flour

⅛ teaspoon salt

FOR THE FILLING

8 ounces cream cheese, at room temperature

¾ cup granulated sugar

3 large eggs, at room temperature

1 cup half-and-half

1 teaspoon vanilla extract

2 tablespoons grated lemon zest

2 cups fresh raspberries, plus extra for serving

Softly whipped cream, for serving

First, make the pie crust: In a large mixing bowl, cream together the butter and brown sugar with an electric mixer until the mixture is light and fluffy. Then gradually add the beaten egg, mixing until just incorporated. In a separate bowl, sift together the flour and salt. Add the flour mixture to the creamed mixture all at once, and mix just until the dough forms a ball. Flatten the dough into a disk, cover it with plastic wrap, and refrigerate for 20 minutes or until it is firm.

Have a 9-inch tart pan with removable bottom ready. On a lightly floured surface, roll out the dough to form a 12-inch round that is about ⅛ inch thick. Lightly roll the dough around your rolling pin, dusting off any excess flour as you roll, and unroll it over the tart pan. Gently lay the dough in the pan, lightly pressing it into the bottom and up the sides. Roll your rolling pin over the top of the pan to remove any excess dough. With a thumb-up movement, again press the dough into the pan, and then once again roll the rolling pin over the top to remove any extra dough. With a fork, prick the dough in the bottom of the pan. Cover the pan with plastic wrap and refrigerate it for 20 minutes. (This will help chill the butter and rest the gluten in the dough.)

Place the rack in the center of the oven and preheat the oven to 400°F.

recipe continues

Remove the pastry shell from the refrigerator and line it with parchment paper or aluminum foil. Fill the shell with pie weights, rice, or dried beans, making sure the weights reach the top of the pan and are evenly distributed. Bake for 20 to 25 minutes, or until the crust is dry and a light golden brown. Remove the weights and let the crust cool completely on a wire rack.

Reduce the oven temperature to 350°F.

To make the filling, put the cream cheese in a medium mixing bowl and use an electric mixer to beat it until it is smooth. Add the sugar and beat until it is incorporated in the cream cheese. Add the eggs, one at a time, and process until thoroughly combined. Add the half-and-half, vanilla, and lemon zest, and beat until well blended and smooth.

Place the tart pan on a baking sheet. Carefully pour the filling into the cooked tart shell. Arrange the raspberries evenly around the filled tart, and bake for 30 to 35 minutes, or until the filling is set (test by gently shaking the pan). Transfer the tart to a wire rack to cool.

Serve warm or cold, accompanied by softly whipped cream and fresh raspberries. Refrigerate any leftovers.

Two wonderful types of ever-bearing raspberries to grow include the 'Dorman Red' and 'Heritage' varieties. 'Dorman Red' is especially vigorous and productive in the South, where heat and humidity often prevent successful raspberry growing. 'Heritage' raspberries offer huge crops producing classic, medium-size berries with a mild flavor.

SUMMER

WHITE SANGRÍA

I ENJOY ENTERTAINING IN THE SUMMER MONTHS, when my guests can be outside relaxing and enjoying the beauty of the garden. This white sangría goes with that kind of party because it is an immediate mood setter. The recipe produces a delightfully refreshing beverage with a perfect blend of flavors and has been a hit at my cookouts. I like the ease and informality of serving one drink. I greet guests and offer them a filled glass, and then encourage them to get a refill anytime at the "pour your own" drink station, where I have several prepared pitchers of the sangría available.

The drink is a good complement to Black Bean and Spinach Burritos (page 40) and your favorite guacamole and chips. Sangría tastes better if you make it ahead of time, as fruit infuses the wine with its flavor. The way I see it, the more things I can make before the guests arrive, the more time I have to enjoy the party myself. And another plus about this recipe is that you don't have to break the bank on bottles of expensive white wine for a drink that tastes so good.

Scrape the seeds from the vanilla bean, and set the seeds and bean halves aside.

Combine the water, sugar, and the vanilla bean and seeds in a saucepan, and bring to a boil over medium-high heat. Cook, stirring, until the sugar has dissolved completely. Remove the pan from the heat, set the syrup aside, and let it cool completely.

Strain the syrup into a large pitcher, and discard the vanilla bean and seeds. Add all the remaining ingredients, and chill for 1 hour. (Since there is so much fruit, I recommend using a stout pitcher with an open top, or even a punch bowl, so your guests can add fruit to their glasses.)

To serve, pour the sangría over ice.

SERVES 6

1 vanilla bean, split in half lengthwise

½ cup water

½ cup sugar

1 bottle white wine (I prefer Riesling, Pinot Gris, or Pinot Grigio)

1 pint fresh strawberries, hulled and sliced

1 Granny Smith apple, cored and thinly sliced

1 lemon, thinly sliced

1 orange, thinly sliced

1 fresh pineapple, trimmed, peeled, and thinly sliced

2 ounces (¼ cup) peach schnapps

2 ounces (¼ cup) Triple Sec

FRESH PEACH PUNCH

SERVES 16

4 very ripe fresh
   peaches (either cling
   or freestone), peeled
   and sliced

½ cup superfine sugar

½ cup brandy

2 tablespoons finely
   chopped fresh mint
   leaves

2 bottles German Rhine
   wine or Riesling wine

1 quart chilled club soda

Fresh mint sprigs, for
   garnish

THE PEACH IS ONE OF THOSE deliciously wonderful tastes of summer. In an orchard not far from the Garden Home Retreat, there are over fourteen varieties of peaches, each with its own subtle characteristics of flavor, color, and texture. There are two distinct categories of peaches: cling and freestone. The terms refer to whether the seed, or stone, actually tears away from the flesh of the peach. Freestone peaches have a seed that is easily removed; the stone of cling peaches needs to be cut from the fruit. You'll find that even canned peaches indicate these categories on the label.

Cling varieties tend to ripen earlier in the season. They are some of the first peaches you'll find in the market, and their flesh is generally firmer. The freestones ripen later, and they tend to be softer and juicier. They are easy to use in cooking, and peeling and slicing them is a snap. Both are delicious and either can be used in this refreshing punch.

For the best flavor when buying peaches, try to purchase them very close to the day you will be eating them, as they ripen much faster than you think. And if you can't eat them all, try freezing them to use in another season. It's like recapturing the taste of summer.

Combine the peaches, sugar, brandy, and chopped mint in a food processor, and process until the sugar has dissolved. Transfer to a large pitcher or a punch bowl, and add the wine. Chill for 2 to 3 hours.

When ready to serve, add the club soda. Garnish with mint sprigs.

SAVORY GRIT CAKES WITH OVEN-SMOKED TOMATOES

NATCHEZ CHEF REGINA CHARBONEAU shared her recipe for these heavenly grit cakes. Now, if you haven't tried grits in any form, this is a great introduction. Not only do these fun little two-bite cakes look appetizing, they deliver on taste. I also like how they can be used either as make-ahead hors d'oeuvres or as a side dish to accompany a full meal. Try them with the Rubbed Beef Tenderloin (page 212) and the Grilled Summer Salad (page 92).

In my part of the world, how and when you eat grits falls strictly along the lines of honored family traditions and strong opinion. Some have grits for breakfast with only salt, or with gravy, or with sugar, molasses, and butter. Then there are those who love grits when used creatively as a starch with cheese and savory seasonings. Now *this* is the point where you start to get my attention.

I have an uncle who is legendary for his inability to cook. After all, why try when you are married to my aunt, who is supremely talented in the kitchen? He goes near a stove only to warm his hands or to make the one dish he has ever prepared, called "mush," which is boiled cornmeal with salt and butter. For us children, the recipe held little appeal, and today we all laugh about how that's still the only thing he makes when my aunt is not around to have supper ready. We are beginning to build some hope for the man because he can now turn out a mean bowl of grits.

To prepare the grit cakes, bring the broth to a boil in a large saucepan. Slowly add the grits, stirring with a wire whisk to make sure the mixture is smooth. Lower the heat to medium and cook for 5 to 7 minutes, or until the mixture has thickened. Add the salt, butter, cream cheese, rosemary, and garlic. Stir until the grits are smooth.

Pour the mixture into a buttered 10 x 15-inch baking pan and set aside to cool. (The grits can be made a day ahead and refrigerated overnight.) When the grits have cooled and firmed, cut them into rounds with a 1½-inch biscuit cutter, or if you prefer, cut them into approximately 48 squares (cutting the grits into squares leaves no waste!).

recipe continues

SERVES 12

SAVORY GRIT CAKES

2 quarts chicken broth

2 cups quick-cooking grits (5-minute grits)

1 teaspoon salt

8 tablespoons (1 stick) butter, cut into pieces, or 8 tablespoons nondairy spread, at room temperature

8 ounces cream cheese or plain goat cheese, cut into pieces, at room temperature

4 teaspoons finely chopped fresh rosemary leaves

1 teaspoon minced garlic

OVEN-SMOKED TOMATOES

12 Roma (plum) tomatoes

3 tablespoons olive oil

1 tablespoon liquid hickory smoke flavoring

1 teaspoon sea salt

1 tablespoon cracked black pepper

½ teaspoon minced garlic

FOR SERVING

¼ cup finely chopped fresh rosemary leaves (optional)

To prepare the smoked tomatoes, preheat the oven to 300°F. Quarter the tomatoes lengthwise, and place them on a baking sheet. In a small bowl, mix together the olive oil, liquid smoke, sea salt, cracked black pepper, and garlic. Drizzle the mixture over the tomatoes and bake for 30 minutes. Keep warm.

Just before serving, increase the oven temperature to 325°F. Lightly grease a baking sheet with canola oil spray, and place as many grit cakes as will fit on the sheet. Spray the cakes lightly with the canola oil (this will help them brown), and bake for about 15 minutes or until slightly browned. Repeat with the remaining grit cakes if necessary. Keep warm.

To serve, top each cake with a smoked tomato wedge, and if you like, sprinkle the tomato and grit cakes with some finely chopped rosemary. Serve hot.

The word *grits* is a derivative of the Old English word *grytta*, which means a coarse meal of any kind. True to their name, grits are made from corn that has been ground just shy of the consistency of meal. It has been a staple of the Southern diet for more than two hundred years.

BRUSCHETTA THREE WAYS

I'M A TEXTURE PERSON. Next to the flavor of food, texture runs a close second for me. *Crunchy* and *toasty* are two of my favorite words in the culinary lexicon. I'll always reach for the crunchiest, crustiest, crispiest anything. I think this is one of the reasons why I enjoy bruschetta so much. Bruschetta also appeals to my "sweep the floor" approach to cooking. The toasted, olive-oil-anointed bread is the perfect canvas for some delectable, often surprising combinations. This anything-goes technique is all about using what you have and what you can creatively pull together by foraging through the pantry, fridge, and garden.

These three recipes for bruschetta are tasty flavor combinations that marry beautifully with the texture of the bread. Toast the bread first, then add the ingredients, always making sure they are not too juicy, lest the bruschetta become soggy. You could do a second round under the broiler if necessary, but only briefly.

Try these and other creative combinations you come up with to serve at a casual salad and bruschetta party. It's a fun and easy way to entertain a few friends on a weekend.

BASIC BRUSCHETTA

SERVES 8 TO 12

24–26 ¼-inch-thick slices good-quality baguette	¼ cup olive oil 4 to 6 garlic cloves, halved	1 teaspoon sea salt

Preheat the oven to 450°F. Lightly brush both sides of the bread slices with olive oil, and arrange them on a baking sheet. Toast the bread in the oven, turning it as necessary, until both sides are crisp and browned, 3 minutes per side.

Remove the bread from the oven and rub each slice with the cut side of a halved garlic clove, and then sprinkle with a little sea salt. Eat plain or add one of the following toppings.

NOTE: The bruschetta can also be toasted on the grill.

recipe continues

BLUE CHEESE AND FIG TOPPING

½ package (4 ounces) cream cheese, at room temperature

½ cup (2 ounces) crumbled Gorgonzola cheese

36 slices Basic Bruschetta

½ cup fig preserves or jam

Preheat the oven to 350°F.

Stir the cream cheese and Gorgonzola together in a small bowl until well blended. Spread a heaping ½ teaspoon of the cheese mixture onto each piece of bruschetta and top each with a rounded ½ teaspoon of the fig preserves. Arrange the slices on an ungreased baking sheet, and bake on the middle rack of the oven for 8 to 10 minutes, or until thoroughly heated.

GOAT CHEESE AND TOMATO TOPPING

1 cup seeded, chopped plum tomatoes

4 teaspoons chopped fresh oregano leaves

4 teaspoons extra-virgin olive oil

2 teaspoons balsamic vinegar

½ teaspoon salt

¼ teaspoon freshly ground black pepper

½ cup (4 ounces) goat cheese with fine herbs

24 slices Basic Bruschetta

Combine the chopped tomatoes, oregano, olive oil, balsamic vinegar, salt, and pepper in a medium bowl, tossing gently. Let the mixture stand for 15 minutes.

Spread 1½ teaspoons of the goat cheese on each piece of bruschetta slice. Using a slotted spoon, arrange 1 tablespoon of the tomato mixture over the cheese. Serve immediately.

SLOW-ROASTED CHERRY TOMATO TOPPING

3 pints cherry tomatoes, halved

2 tablespoons extra-virgin olive oil

3 garlic cloves, minced

½ teaspoon salt

½ teaspoon freshly ground black pepper

¼ cup sliced fresh basil leaves

1 tablespoon red wine vinegar

24 slices Basic Bruschetta

Anchovy fillets, kalamata olives, or sliced fresh basil leaves, for garnish

Preheat the oven to 325°F.

Toss the tomatoes in a bowl with the oil, garlic, salt, and pepper. Place the tomatoes on a baking sheet and roast for 45 minutes.

Combine the roasted tomatoes with the basil and vinegar. Top the baguette slices with the roasted tomato mixture. Garnish with your choice of anchovy fillets, kalamata olives, or sliced fresh basil.

TOMATO HERB SOUP

WHEN THE FIRST TOMATOES BEGIN TO RIPEN on the vine, it heralds a period of great garden abundance. Once they start, I can hardly keep up with them. And since few items are so greatly anticipated for their juicy goodness, it's a gardening sin to let any go to waste.

This recipe for tomato herb soup is one of the many ways I use my fresh tomatoes. In fact, if you are overrun with tomatoes and a few become a bit overripe, this is a great way to use them. The soup can be made ahead of time and kept in the refrigerator—or for that matter, in the freezer for winter. I like to use the big tomatoes, such as beefsteak or 'Big Boy', but any size tomato will serve the purpose quite well. Sometimes a medley makes for interesting flavor combinations: meaty plum tomatoes are dense and rich in flavor, and a few yellow tomatoes will influence the color of the soup. Fresh thyme and basil are natural companions to tomatoes in whatever form they are prepared.

SERVES 8

12 tablespoons (1½ sticks) unsalted butter

2 tablespoons extra-virgin olive oil

1 large onion, thinly sliced

8 fresh thyme sprigs, leaves removed

8 large fresh basil leaves, chopped

Salt and freshly ground black pepper, to taste

2½ pounds fresh tomatoes, peeled and cored

3 tablespoons tomato paste

⅓ cup all-purpose flour

1 quart chicken broth

1 cup heavy (whipping) cream

Croutons, for garnish

Melt 8 tablespoons of the butter in a large saucepan, and mix in the olive oil. Then add the onions, thyme leaves, basil, and salt and pepper. Cook over medium heat, stirring occasionally, until the onions have wilted, about 5 minutes. Add the tomatoes and tomato paste, and stir to blend. Bring the mixture to a simmer, and continue to simmer for 10 minutes.

Place the flour in small mixing bowl and add 5 tablespoons of the broth, stirring to blend. Combine the flour mixture with the tomato mixture. Then add the remaining broth and simmer for 30 minutes, stirring frequently to prevent scorching.

Ladle the soup into a food processor and puree until smooth. Return the soup to the saucepan, and add the cream. Bring to a simmer, stirring occasionally. Mix in the remaining 4 tablespoons butter. The soup can be served either hot or cold, garnished with croutons.

SHRIMP BISQUE

SERVES 4 TO 6

3 tablespoons olive oil

2 cups chopped leeks, white and tender light green parts

1 tablespoon chopped garlic

Pinch of cayenne pepper

1 pound large shrimp, peeled and deveined, shells reserved for the Seafood Stock

⅓ cup cognac or brandy

⅓ cup dry sherry

4 tablespoons (½ stick) butter

¼ cup all-purpose flour

2 cups half-and-half

4 cups Seafood Stock (recipe follows)

⅓ cup tomato paste

½ teaspoon kosher salt, or to taste

½ teaspoon freshly ground black pepper, or to taste

MY FRIEND TERI MAKES THIS BISQUE, and it always gets accolades from guests. Having grandparents from Louisiana has affected her culinary sensibilities!

Shrimp is in its prime during summer, but it is a treat any time of the year. As a child I visited friends in Biloxi during the blessing of the shrimp fleet, an impressive armada of fishing boats and a lot of Catholic regalia bobbing around in the Gulf. We brought ice chests full of shrimp back home with us, which we enjoyed until we hurt. No one even considered freezing such a delicacy. Today, however, good-quality frozen shrimp is readily available.

Heat the olive oil in a large pot or Dutch oven over medium-low heat. Add the leeks and cook for 10 minutes, or until they are tender but not browned. Add the garlic and cook for 1 more minute. Add the cayenne pepper and the shrimp, and cook over medium to low heat for 3 minutes, stirring occasionally. Add the cognac and cook for 1 minute; then add the sherry and cook for 3 minutes longer. Transfer the shrimp mixture to a food processor fitted with the steel blade, and pulse until coarsely pureed.

Melt the butter in the same pot. Add the flour and cook over medium-low heat for 1 minute, stirring with a wooden spoon. Add the half-and-half and cook, stirring with a whisk, until thickened, about 3 minutes. Stir in the pureed shrimp mixture, the stock, and the tomato paste, salt, and pepper. Heat gently until hot but not boiling. Season to taste, and serve hot.

SEAFOOD STOCK

MAKE THIS STOCK on the day you plan to use it.

Shrimp shells from 1 pound shrimp

4 cups cold water

1 tablespoon black peppercorns

1 onion, chopped

1 celery rib, chopped

1 bay leaf

Rinse the shrimp shells and place them in a large pot. Add the cold water and bring to a simmer. Add the peppercorns, onions, celery, and bay leaf and continue to simmer gently for up to 40 minutes. (Don't leave the stock simmering for longer than 40 minutes, as it could become bitter.) Strain, and cool or use immediately.

COOL CUCUMBER SOUP

CUCUMBERS PREPARED AS SOUP is one of my favorite ways to enjoy this distinctly summer vegetable. When the temperature starts to rise, the cucumber vine kicks into high gear in the garden and pumps out cukes faster than you can use them, second only to zucchini in productivity! This soup can easily be made a day ahead, or on a weekend to enjoy during the week, so while you're at it, whip up an extra batch.

Slicing cucumbers, also known as table cucumbers, are usually served raw in salads, sandwiches, drinks, soups, sushi, and hors d'oeuvres to add crunch, but they can also be cooked like zucchini. Pickling cucumbers are usually smaller than slicing cucumbers, and often have thicker, bumpy skins. They're hard to find in supermarkets, but you can often obtain them during the summer months in farmers' markets—or better still, you can grow your own.

For this recipe I use English cucumbers, which are the extra-long table variety found in supermarkets. They are seedless, so they are a good choice for soup. I grow 'Straight Eight', which is equally delicious. It is a vigorous and productive plant that produces dark green, blunt-ended, cylindrical, seven- to eight-inch-long fruits; I remove the seeds if they are prominent.

Peel and coarsely chop the cucumbers. On a small chopping board, crush the garlic and ¼ teaspoon of the salt together to form a paste, using the flat side of a chef's knife. Combine the cucumbers, garlic, remaining 1¼ teaspoons salt, chopped green onions, and the buttermilk in a blender and process until completely smooth. Add the dill and parsley, and pulse several times to combine. Transfer the soup to a bowl, cover, and refrigerate for 1 hour or until thoroughly chilled.

Before serving, season the soup with salt and pepper to taste, and add the lemon juice. Divide it among four soup bowls, garnish with fresh dill and parsley, and serve.

SERVES 4

Two 14- to 16-ounce English (seedless) cucumbers

½ garlic clove, minced

1½ teaspoons kosher salt, plus more to taste

2 small green onions, white and green parts, chopped

2 cups buttermilk, or 1 cup milk plus 1 cup sour cream

1 tablespoon minced fresh dill leaves

1 teaspoon minced fresh flat-leaf parsley leaves

Freshly ground black pepper, to taste

Juice of ½ lemon

Fresh dill and parsley, for garnish

THE GARDEN SANDWICH

SERVES 4

FOR THE VINAIGRETTE

4 teaspoons chopped
   mixed fresh herbs

2 teaspoons olive oil

¼ cup champagne
   vinegar

2 teaspoons Dijon
   mustard

1 teaspoon kosher salt

1 teaspoon cracked
   black pepper

**FOR THE HERBED GOAT
CHEESE**

2 teaspoons finely
   chopped fresh mixed
   herbs

½ teaspoon freshly
   ground black pepper

¼ teaspoon kosher salt

4 ounces plain goat
   cheese, at room
   temperature

FOR THE SANDWICH

¼ pound fresh greens,
   such as baby lettuce,
   beet tops, radish
   tops, and chard

Artisanal bread, such as
   a "rustic" loaf, about
   12 inches long

Meaty plum tomatoes,
   cored and sliced

1 cucumber, peeled and
   thinly sliced

1 green bell pepper,
   thinly sliced

1 red onion, thinly sliced

Salt and freshly ground
   black pepper

THIS RECIPE TAKES FULL ADVANTAGE OF FRESH HERBS. There really are few excuses for someone not to grow their own—most herbs are quite content in containers with just about 6 hours of sun. So even if you only have a sliver of space, you can easily grow them on a doorstep or windowsill, snip their leaves, and add their flavors to your favorite recipes.

I'd encourage you to start early in the season with herbs that thrive in the cool temperatures of spring, such as parsley (both flat-leaf and curly), chives, and cilantro. As it warms up, add rosemary, thyme, dill, and some of those exquisite basils, such as 'Lettuce leaf', sweet, and 'Purple Ruffles'.

With a small sampling of various herbs, you can brighten the flavor of this dressing and make the most delicious herbed goat cheese. (For a shortcut, feel free to substitute a prepared herbed goat cheese.) When these are combined with fresh spring greens from the garden and some crusty bread, it is sensational. Any bread is fine, but I prefer a rustic loaf or a fresh baguette. Here's my secret: I pull a bit of the bread out of the center and leave the crust, so there is a higher crust-to-bread ratio. This gives me added room for the goat cheese and other delights. I also like to pile on some baby beet greens and thinly sliced radishes; really, anything goes.

Combine all the vinaigrette ingredients in a jar. Cover tightly and shake vigorously.

Combine all ingredients for the herbed goat cheese; mix well.

Toss the sandwich greens in a bowl with just enough vinaigrette to coat. Slice the bread lengthwise and remove part of the inside of the loaf. Spread each cut side with the herbed goat cheese. Then layer the bottom half with the tomatoes, cucumbers, peppers, and onions. Season the vegetables with salt and pepper to taste. Top with the vinaigrette-coated greens. Add the upper half of the bread, slice, and serve.

GARDEN TOMATO SALAD

THERE HAS BEEN A LOT OF TALK about the way tomatoes used to taste and how much better they were. I disagree! Actually, they're better now. Let's face it, our grandparents grew a single variety, or maybe two, of tomatoes and that was it. Today tomatoes enjoy greater acknowledgment and celebration than they did when first introduced in Europe in the fifteenth century. What few people realize is that while Americans have an all-consuming love affair with tomatoes today, the relationship got off to a rocky start—in fact, they were believed to be poisonous!

I am overjoyed with our deepening appreciation for tomatoes—both heirloom and some of the newer hybrid varieties. The greater the diversity the better. I grow as many varieties as I can and am constantly on the hunt to find more. Serving a platter of thinly sliced mixed tomatoes with some seasonal garden bedfellows such as green onions, basil, and basil flowers makes a feast for the eyes and the taste buds.

Combine the vegetable oil, vinegar, parsley, green onions, garlic, salt, dill, basil, and pepper in a small bowl or a jar, and whisk or shake until well mixed. Cut the tomatoes into ½-inch-thick slices and arrange them in a serving dish. Pour the dressing over the top. Chill, covered, for 2 hours, basting occasionally, before serving.

During colonial times, folklore had it that if you ate a tomato, it would poison you. So instead of using them for food, the colonists grew tomatoes purely for decoration. In 1830, Colonel Robert Gibbon Johnson set out to prove that they were perfectly safe to eat, so he filled a basket and began eating them on the steps of the local courthouse. When he didn't expire, tomatoes were deemed edible, though mostly in a highly processed form, after being thoroughly cooked with vinegar and spices. Ketchup was popular long before salad tomatoes caught on.

SERVES 6

⅔ cup vegetable oil

¼ cup red wine vinegar

2 teaspoons chopped fresh flat-leaf parsley leaves

2 green onions, white and green parts, thinly sliced

1 garlic clove, minced

1 teaspoon salt

1 teaspoon finely chopped fresh dill leaves

1 teaspoon finely chopped fresh basil leaves

¼ teaspoon freshly ground black pepper

4 medium tomatoes (a colorful variety, if available)

GRILLED SUMMER SALAD

SERVES 8 TO 10

FOR THE SALAD

¼ cup pine nuts

6 to 8 fresh poblano
   chiles

8 Roma tomatoes

2 medium green bell
   peppers

2 medium red bell
   peppers

8 garlic cloves,
   unpeeled

**CUMIN AND
CORIANDER DRESSING**

¼ cup olive oil

1½ teaspoons grated
   lemon zest

3 tablespoons fresh
   lemon juice

1 teaspoon salt, or to
   taste

½ teaspoon ground
   cumin

½ teaspoon ground
   coriander

¼ teaspoon freshly
   ground black pepper,
   or to taste

1 tablespoon tiny
   capers, drained
   (optional)

THE NOTION OF GRILLING VEGETABLES is a relatively recent idea. For a long time the grill was a man's domain, and the grill was all about meat—*red* meat! Grilling vegetables would have people talking! This salad is a compendium of what's coming out of the garden, but make your own medley of what you like: peppers, tomatoes, eggplant, zucchini—all grilled and served together in all their grilled glory.

Romas, also known as paste tomatoes, generally have a thicker fruit wall, fewer seeds, and a denser, grainier flesh than other tomatoes. Romas also tend to be oblong in shape and heavy for their size. They are a good choice for this salad because they are meaty and grill well. Fresh poblano chiles, often mislabeled *pasillas,* are easy to identify because they are very dark green. If you can't find poblanos, use green New Mexico chiles, which are also called California or Anaheim chiles.

When grilling vegetables, just remember to put a little olive oil on them and not to be in a big hurry. Keep the fire hot but not to the point that you're charring the vegetables. The idea of cooking them outside is to have the veggies take on as much of the flavor and aroma of the grill as possible.

Toast the pine nuts in a dry skillet over medium-high heat, stirring them occasionally, until lightly browned, about 5 minutes. Set them aside.

Preheat an outdoor grill to medium-high heat (or preheat the broiler).

Arrange the poblanos, tomatoes, bell peppers, and garlic on a greased grill rack, and grill (or broil) 5 inches from the heat source until the vegetable skins crack and char; don't allow them to become mushy. Place the charred vegetables in a bowl, cover it with plastic wrap, and let cool for 10 minutes. Then peel, seed, and coarsely chop the poblanos, tomatoes, and bell peppers. Peel and mash the garlic. Combine the poblanos, tomatoes, peppers, and garlic in a nonreactive salad bowl (glass or plastic), and toss. Let stand for 1 hour or longer to allow the flavors to blend. The salad may be served immediately or can be prepared up to 1 day in advance and stored in the refrigerator. Let it stand at room temperature for 30 minutes before adding the dressing.

To prepare the dressing, combine the olive oil, lemon zest and juice, salt, cumin, coriander, pepper, and capers (if using) in a small bowl, and whisk until well mixed.

To serve, pour the dressing over the salad and toss to coat well.

VARIATION
PASTA SALAD
SERVES 12 TO 14

For a delicious pasta salad, cook 12 ounces small pasta, such as farfalle or penne, according to the package directions. Toss the pasta with the grilled vegetables and a double recipe of the Cumin and Coriander Dressing.

Both poblano and green New Mexico chiles are mild in flavor and rank near the bottom of the Scoville scale; if you want to add a bit more kick to your salad, consider the hotter 'Serrano' or cayenne peppers.

NIÇOISE SALAD

FOR THE SALAD

8 skinless, boneless
 heritage chicken
 breasts

Olive oil

Salt and freshly ground
 black pepper

4 red potatoes,
 unpeeled

1 pound asparagus,
 trimmed

8 cups mixed salad
 greens, rinsed
 thoroughly and
 patted dry

8 hard-cooked eggs,
 sliced

8 vine-ripened
 tomatoes, each cut
 into 4 wedges

1 cucumber, peeled and
 thinly sliced

1 red onion, thinly sliced

24 large green olives,
 pitted

Kosher salt

Freshly cracked black
 pepper

FOR THE DRESSING

¼ cup champagne
 vinegar

1 tablespoon Dijon
 mustard

3 tablespoons small
 capers, drained

1 teaspoon kosher salt

½ teaspoon freshly
 cracked black pepper

½ cup extra-virgin
 olive oil

THIS RECIPE IS A LOCAL INTERPRETATION of an old French standby. It captures a moment in the garden when there are plenty of freshly dug potatoes and the laying hens are producing eggs at full tilt.

I grow lots of different varieties of potatoes. One of my favorites is the Kennebec. It was also one of my grandfather Smith's favorite varieties. He always dug his potatoes on the Fourth of July. As a little guy, this made an impression on me—not only because of the date, but also because of his method. He used his two mules, Kit and Belle, to pull the plow that turned the potatoes out of the ground. Talk about a memory from a bygone era!

Signature ingredients of Niçoise salad include potatoes, eggs, and olives, but I also like to add other seasonal favorites to the lettuce, such as asparagus and beet greens. Really, anything goes . . . certainly anchovies for the purist. Even if I don't have every item on hand, it doesn't keep me from making this salad. I like it because you can be creative. Sometimes I prepare part of it ahead of time and add more ingredients to the platter or individual plates just before people arrive. It is a great salad if you are entertaining several guests.

Preheat the oven to 350°F.
 Rub the chicken breasts with olive oil, place them in a baking dish, and season them with salt and pepper. Bake until they are just cooked through (they should still be very juicy), 25 to 30 minutes. Remove the chicken from the baking dish, and when it has cooled slightly, thinly slice it on the diagonal. Set the chicken aside.

Bring a large saucepan of salted water to a boil. Fill a large, wide bowl with ice and cold water, and set it aside.

Add the potatoes to the boiling water, and cook until just tender, 15 to 20 minutes, depending on their size. Drain, and submerge the potatoes in the ice water. When they have cooled completely, remove the potatoes with a slotted spoon (reserving the ice water) and cut them into ¼-inch-thick slices. Set the potatoes aside.

Fill a skillet with salted water and bring it to a boil. Reduce the heat, add the asparagus, and simmer for 1 minute. Then immediately remove the asparagus and submerge them in the same bowl of ice water. When they have cooled completely, drain and pat dry.

To assemble the salad, divide the salad greens among eight plates. Around the outside of the greens, arrange the asparagus, sliced egg, tomato wedges, sliced cucumber, sliced onion, olives, and potato slices. Sprinkle with kosher salt and cracked black pepper.

Combine all the dressing ingredients, except the olive oil, in a large bowl and whisk to combine. Slowly drizzle the olive oil into the mixture, whisking to combine. Drizzle the vinaigrette dressing over the greens. Place the sliced chicken in the middle of the greens, and drizzle the chicken with a little of the dressing. Serve immediately.

ZUCCHINI AND LEMON SALAD

SERVES 6 TO 8

3 or 4 medium zucchini, unpeeled, ends trimmed, cut into matchsticks (4 cups)

Grated zest and juice of 1 lemon

1 tablespoon chopped fresh mint leaves

1 tablespoon chopped fresh dill leaves

6 ounces feta cheese, crumbled

2 tablespoons extra-virgin olive oil

1 teaspoon salt

1 teaspoon freshly ground black pepper

IF THERE WERE AN AWARD for overachieving vegetables, zucchini would take the top prize, hands down. Because of its fecundity, cooks have done their best to capitalize on its abundant nature and have created a myriad of ways to use it.

Zucchini is best when it's fresh, so seize the summer season while the garden and farmers' markets runneth over with it. I don't preserve it by drying or canning it, but I do freeze it when it is young (lightly blanched). It can be frozen either whole or sliced, and will last for about 6 months. I recommend using one of the vacuum-pack sealers for the best results.

This salad is one of the many ways I've come to enjoy the flavor of fresh zucchini. While not a heavy-tasting vegetable, in this dish it is made even lighter and fresher with the flavor of lemon. The salad is an agreeable companion to grilled pork or chicken.

In a large bowl, combine the zucchini with the lemon zest, juice, mint, dill, feta, and olive oil. Toss the ingredients gently to mix, and season with the salt and pepper.

Cover, and refrigerate for at least 2 hours and up to 24 hours before serving.

FRESH CORN SALAD

WHEN YOU PREPARE THIS SALAD, do yourself a favor and find the freshest corn you can. And please, don't boil the corn: steam it instead. This helps hold in the sweetness and retain some of the crunch in the kernel. If you want corn mush, boil some cornmeal!

This recipe yields generous portions and is great for large gatherings or summer potlucks. The salad is fresh, light, sweet, and cool, so it makes the perfect complement to grilled and barbecue dishes.

Shuck the corn, and remove the silk.

Steam the corn in a deep vegetable steamer for about 10 minutes, until crisp-tender.

Standing an ear of corn vertically on a cutting board and using a sharp knife, slice off the kernels, cutting from top to bottom. (Avoid dragging the knife over the cob once the kernels are cut; you do not want to "milk the cob" of the remaining corn juice because this would cloud the clarity of the salad.) You should have 4 cups of corn kernels.

In a large bowl, combine the corn with the remaining vegetables, black beans, and parsley, gently folding them together.

In a small bowl, whisk together the dressing ingredients. Pour the dressing over the salad and fold it in gently.

The salad can be served immediately at room temperature or refrigerated up to 5 days and served cold.

SERVES 10 TO 16

FOR THE SALAD

6 ears fresh sweet corn

2 cups diced fresh tomatoes

½ cup diced red onion

½ cup diced red bell pepper

1 15-ounce can black beans, rinsed and drained

1 tablespoon chopped fresh flat-leaf parsley leaves

FOR THE DRESSING

¼ cup extra-virgin olive oil

1 tablespoon red wine vinegar

Juice of 1 lemon

1 large garlic clove, finely minced

1½ teaspoons kosher salt

½ teaspoon freshly cracked black pepper

When choosing corn from the farmer's market, pick ears with plump little kernels and sticky silks, all indications the corn has been freshly picked and is ready to eat. I press kernels with my thumbnail to see the juice fly—the juicier the fresher!

OVEN-FRIED CATFISH WITH FRESH DILL TARTAR SAUCE

CHILDREN WHO VISIT THE GARDEN HOME RETREAT love to go to the catfish pond to watch the fish rise to the surface to gobble up their floating food.

To keep a good population balance in the pond, we need to fish out a few catfish each month or so. While deep-fried catfish is a Southern signature dish, I like it oven-fried, which is a bit lighter, with the fresh dill tartar sauce.

SERVES 4 TO 6

8 4-ounce catfish fillets
1 teaspoon salt
2 tablespoons hot sauce
Vegetable cooking spray
1 cup yellow cornmeal
1½ teaspoons kosher salt
½ teaspoon freshly ground black pepper
Tartar Sauce (recipe follows)

Sprinkle the catfish fillets with the salt, and place them in a heavy-duty zip-top plastic bag. Add the hot sauce, seal, and chill for 2 hours, turning the bag over occasionally.

Preheat the oven to 425°F. Coat a baking sheet with vegetable cooking spray. Mix the cornmeal, kosher salt, and pepper together in a shallow bowl.

Remove the fillets from the marinade, and dredge them in the seasoned cornmeal. Place the fish on the baking sheet, and bake for 10 to 15 minutes, or until the fish flakes with a fork. Then turn on the broiler, and broil the fillets 3 inches from the heat (with the oven door partially open) for 4 minutes, or until lightly browned. Serve with the Tartar Sauce on the side.

TARTAR SAUCE

MAKES 1¼ CUPS

1 cup good-quality mayonnaise (such as Hellmann's)
1½ tablespoons finely chopped zesty dill pickles

1½ tablespoons small capers, drained
1 tablespoon finely chopped shallots
1 teaspoon grated lemon zest

1 teaspoon finely chopped fresh dill leaves
1 tablespoon fresh lemon juice

Stir all the ingredients together in a small bowl. Cover and chill for at least 2 hours before serving.

GRILLED CHICKEN BREASTS WITH WHITE BARBECUE SAUCE

SERVES 8

1 cup good-quality mayonnaise (such as Hellmann's)

3 tablespoons distilled white vinegar

1 tablespoon freshly cracked black pepper

8 boneless, skinless heritage chicken breasts

WHO SAYS BARBECUE SAUCE HAS TO BE RED, or even tomato-based? I know that in my part of the world, the idea of serving barbecue sauce in any other color but red is heresy and can get you into a lot of hot water in a hurry. Some people don't have much of an open mind when it comes to the cult of barbecue.

So, when I served this white barbecue sauce at a recent family gathering, I had several relatives doing double takes and asking, "What is this?" But once they tasted it, they had to agree that it was a nice change. I knew I had won them over when I had calls the next day asking for the recipe. This really is a light and refreshing change from the usual grilled summer chicken. Try it with Fresh Corn Salad (page 97) and Field Peas with Red Tomato Relish (page 110).

Preheat an outdoor grill to medium-high heat.

In a small bowl, whisk the mayonnaise, vinegar, and pepper together. Set aside half of the mixture to use as a sauce at the table. Brush the remaining mixture over both sides of the chicken breasts. Grill until the chicken is well done, and serve with the reserved barbecue sauce.

GREEK ZUCCHINI PIE

HERE'S ANOTHER GREAT RECIPE for using the zucchini that may be taking over your garden. Even if you don't grow it, in the summer you'll find that zucchini is fresh, inexpensive, and abundant in the farmers' markets. It is best when it is tender and young.

When making this pie, be mindful that because the zucchini adds so much moisture, you'll want to serve it within 30 minutes or so once it comes out of the oven so the phyllo crust remains crispy. This dish is divine with the Garden Tomato Salad (page 91) and a nice dry white wine. Try it. I think you'll agree that it makes a satisfying meal.

Grate the zucchini into a large colander. Sprinkle salt generously over the grated zucchini, and set the colander aside for 30 minutes to allow the zucchini to drain.

Place the zucchini in a large clean dish towel, and squeeze out as much of the excess moisture as possible.

Heat ½ cup olive oil in a large skillet over medium-low heat, and cook the onions and green onions until they are soft, about 7 minutes. Then add the zucchini, ½ teaspoon salt, and cracked pepper to taste, and cook until the excess liquid evaporates, 18 to 25 minutes.

Meanwhile, preheat the oven to 400°F. Combine the feta, dill, and parsley in a bowl, and set it aside.

Separate out 6 sheets of phyllo, and brush them with olive oil on both sides. If the remaining pastry seems to be a bit dry, lay it between two damp kitchen towels.

Place the sheets of phyllo in a 10 x 15-inch baking dish, one oiled sheet layered on top of the next, allowing the dough to hang over the edge of the pan—approximately 2 inches all the way around (enough to be able to fold a little over the zucchini mixture).

Spread half of the zucchini mixture evenly over the phyllo; then scatter half of the feta-herb mixture evenly over the zucchini. In a small bowl, beat the eggs and cream together; drizzle half of this on top of the feta mixture.

recipe continues

SERVES 10 TO 12

2 pounds zucchini (approximately 9 small or 6 medium zucchini)

Salt

⅔ cup olive oil

1 large onion, chopped

4 green onions, white and green parts, chopped

Freshly cracked black pepper

10 ounces feta cheese, crumbled

¼ cup finely chopped fresh dill leaves

¼ cup finely chopped fresh flat-leaf parsley leaves

1 16-ounce package phyllo dough, thawed if frozen

3 eggs, lightly beaten

½ cup heavy cream

Milk, for glazing the crust

Sesame seeds, for garnish

Oil both sides of 6 more sheets of phyllo, and repeat all the layers: phyllo, the remaining zucchini mixture, the remaining herbed feta cheese, the egg-cream mixture.

Finish with 6 more phyllo sheets on top, lightly brushing each with oil. Snip off most of the excess pastry around the edges, leaving just enough to tuck in all the way around the pan. Glaze the pie by brushing the phyllo with a little milk, and scatter sesame seeds on top. Prick the pastry all over with a fork.

Put the pie in the oven and bake for about 1 hour, until it is set (you can shake the pan to see if there is much movement). When the pie is set and the pastry is golden, remove it from the oven. Put a kitchen towel over the top and leave it to cool for 30 minutes before you cut it into squares and serve.

Did you know that you can grow zucchini in containers? Choose the classic 'Black Beauty' variety and simply pick when the fruits are small for "baby zucchini," or try a more compact variety such as the 'Ronde de Nice'. This summer vegetable produces a small plant with large yellow flowers that develop into round, green and cream-speckled fruits. The flavor is best when the zucchini are 1 to 3 inches in diameter.

Look for other late spring and summer recipes using zucchini: Grilled Pork Chops with Zucchini and Peppers (page 42), Zucchini and Lemon Salad (page 96) and Aunt Genny's Zucchini Nut Bread (page 124).

ROSEMARY-GARLIC SMOKED PORK TENDERLOIN

THE NAME OF THIS DISH tells you about the taste you can expect—and it is very flavorful indeed. It has that wonderful combination of rosemary conspiring with garlic, along with the smoke flavor from the grill, all infusing the tenderloin. My goodness! What could be better? You can add to this medley of flavors some good side dish companions, such as the Garden Tomato Salad (page 91) and Aunt Antha's Corn Pudding (page 113). Now, one point of caution: don't overcook the tenderloin. You want it to remain juicy.

SERVES 8 TO 10

4 cups applewood or hickory wood chips

1 2- to 3-pound boneless pork tenderloin

2 tablespoons snipped fresh rosemary leaves

1 tablespoon olive oil

4 garlic cloves, minced

½ teaspoon freshly ground black pepper

¼ teaspoon salt

4 fresh rosemary sprigs

½ lemon

About an hour before grilling time, soak the wood chips in enough water to cover them.

Preheat a charcoal grill to medium-low heat. Drain the wood chips.

Trim the fat from the meat. Combine the snipped rosemary, olive oil, garlic, pepper, and salt in a small bowl. Sprinkle this rub evenly over the meat, and use your fingers to work it in.

Arrange the charcoal around a drip pan. Pour 1 inch of water into the drip pan. Test for medium-low heat above the pan. (Hold your hand, palm side down, in the place where the meat will cook. Count "one thousand one, one thousand two," etc. Being able to keep your hand there for a count of five is equal to medium-low.) Sprinkle half of the wood chips over the coals, and then sprinkle the rosemary sprigs over the chips. Place the meat on a grill rack over the drip pan. Cover, and grill for 1 to 1¼ hours, or until a meat thermometer registers 155°F. Add the remaining wood chips halfway through grilling.

Remove the meat from the grill, and squeeze lemon juice over the meat. Cover with foil and let it stand for 10 minutes before slicing and serving.

For cooking the meat on a gas grill, preheat the grill. Reduce the heat to medium-low. Adjust for indirect cooking, following the manufacturer's directions. Grill as described, but with the meat placed on a rack in a roasting pan.

OH-SO-SWEET ROOT VEGETABLES

THE ONSET OF SUMMER signals the harvest of fresh root vegetables such as potatoes, beets, carrots, radishes, and turnips. They are by definition plants whose edible parts grow underground. Whether I harvest root vegetables by pulling them by their tops from the soil, as I do for radishes and beets, or by digging them out of the ground with a garden fork, it's always a delightful surprise to see these beauties come to the surface like buried treasure.

Root vegetables tend to have similar growing requirements and do best in cool weather. Since they are hardy, I plant them early in the spring and harvest them in June and through the summer. This medley of roasted vegetables captures their prime freshness. Sometimes I like to leave the carrot and turnip tops attached, to add to the presentation.

Serve this delicious mix of many summer vegetables with meat or fish.

SERVES 8 TO 10

1 pound new potatoes
1 pound new carrots
1 pound large radishes
1 pound new turnips
12 garlic cloves
½ cup olive oil
Kosher salt and freshly
   ground black pepper,
   to taste
¼ cup finely chopped
   fresh thyme leaves

Preheat the oven to 450°F.

Wash the vegetables. Leave the carrots and radishes whole, but cut the potatoes and turnips so that they are approximately the same size as the carrots and radishes (and therefore will cook in about the same length of time).

Combine the vegetables and garlic in a heavy roasting pan. Add the olive oil and toss to coat; season well with salt and pepper. Roast for about 30 minutes, stirring every 10 minutes, until lightly browned and tender. Gently stir in the chopped thyme during the last 10 minutes of cooking. Add more salt and pepper, if necessary, and serve.

When buying root crops, select firm, unwrinkled vegetables that are relatively heavy in relation to their size. That indicates that the vegetable is fresh. The green tops of turnips and beets can be eaten. Store roots and tubers, unwashed, with their leaves removed, in a cool, dark place for up to 2 weeks. Store leaves in the vegetable crisper of the refrigerator for up to 1 week.

FIELD PEAS WITH RED TOMATO RELISH

SERVES 6

3 slices bacon, cut in
  half, or 6 slices salt
  pork

3 cups shelled field peas
  (such as lady peas or
  black-eyed peas) or
  lima beans

3 green onions, white
  and green parts,
  chopped

Kosher salt and coarsely
  ground black pepper,
  to taste

Grandma Mills's Red
  Tomato Relish (recipe
  follows)

THIS RECIPE CAN BE ADAPTED to any of the great field peas we enjoy during the height of summer. Field peas, or cow peas as they are sometimes called, are part of a noble family of plants that have served both mankind and livestock for centuries. High in protein, these peas are shelled either fresh or dry from long pods. My father's favorite was the tiny lady pea, also called a cream pea. If you ever see these in the grocery store or farmers' market my advice is to buy them all—or at least call me so I can buy them! Sadly, they are rarely grown these days. However, the markets do offer a range of other field peas, such as purple hulls, crowders, black-eyed, and butter peas. I'm sure there are others, but these have always been the main staples in the southern parts of the country.

My friend Teri's grandmother was from Louisiana and always made tomato relish in the summer, which we would have with peas when visiting Teri. This relish is a delicious example of a range of condiments often called chow-chow. Peas came to table with the unspoken expectation that they would be accompanied by any number of these regional variations on the same theme.

Before television (was there such a time?), people would sit on the porch or in the kitchen and shell peas while they listened to the radio. I remember staying with my grandparents when I was small, and Ma Smith would shell peas Saturday night after supper. Around 8 p.m. or so, she would stop and get out her large washtub right there in the kitchen and fill it with warm water so I could have a bath before bedtime. The next day was filled with going to church and visiting nearby relatives. Those certainly were simpler times. A generous serving of peas and tomato relish, along with a nice big slice of warm cornbread, brings back those memories and makes for a fine supper.

In a medium-size pot, cook the bacon over medium heat until browned and crisp. Leaving the bacon and the fat in the pot, add the peas and enough water to cover them by about 1 inch. Bring the water to a boil; then reduce the heat and simmer for 20 minutes. Add the green onions, and season with salt and pepper. Continue to simmer for another 5 to 10 minutes, until the peas are tender but not mushy. Serve with Grandma Mills's Red Tomato Relish.

recipe continues

GRANDMA MILLS'S RED TOMATO RELISH

MAKES 7 TO 8 PINTS

22 medium tomatoes

6 medium onions, chopped

1 cup chopped green bell peppers

4 large garlic cloves, finely chopped

1 teaspoon freshly ground black pepper

1 teaspoon ground cloves

1 teaspoon ground ginger

1½ teaspoons kosher salt

3 cups sugar

1½ cups distilled white vinegar

Bring a large pot of water to a boil. Using tongs, dunk the tomatoes in the water for 30 seconds to blanch them. Allow the tomatoes to cool until they can be handled, and then remove the skins. Once all the tomatoes have been skinned, coarsely chop them (see Note).

Put the tomatoes, onions, and bell peppers in a canning pot or a large stockpot. Add the garlic and cook over medium heat for 1 hour, stirring occasionally.

Remove the pot from the heat and drain off some liquid if necessary. Add the ground pepper, cloves, ginger, salt, sugar, and vinegar. Stir well, and simmer until slightly thick, 25 to 35 minutes.

Ladle the relish into hot, sterile 1-pint canning jars, and seal with the lids and rings, following the manufacturer's directions. Serve the relish at room temperature. After opening the canned relish, store partial jars in the refrigerator.

NOTE: As I chop the blanched tomatoes, I drain off the fresh tomato juice for another use, such as in soup or pasta sauce, or just for drinking! Draining the tomatoes at this point lets you avoid having to drain off extra liquid after cooking them.

How Many Tomatoes in a Pound?

One pound of tomatoes will yield about 1 cup of pulp after peeling and seeding.

Beefsteak	½ to 1 per pound
'Better Boy'	2 to 3 per pound
'Big Boy'	3 to 4 per pound
'Early Girl'	3 to 4 per pound
'Pixie'	30 per pound
Roma	8 per pound

AUNT ANTHA'S
CORN PUDDING

THERE'S A SAYING that anticipation is the greater part of pleasure, but when it comes to sweet corn it is just the opposite. I think waiting for those first home-grown ears to be ready is downright painful! The pleasure comes in sinking your teeth into those yellow nuggets of sweet delight. If precious gold had a taste, this would be it.

In my younger days, I'd often be sent to the garden to check on the progress of the corn. Once there, I'd pull back just a little of the husk from the top of the ears to see how the kernels were developing. Each day they would grow a little larger, but it seemed like it took forever. I made all those trips to the field only to return with the report that the corn wasn't ready. So on the day I found the ears to be just right, I stripped an ear from the stalk, shucked off the husk, and ate it raw, right there in the field! (I did my best to avoid the silks and worms, of course.) Now that was the best ear of sweet corn I ever had.

Sweet corn is one of the signature foods of the American summer, and that fact hasn't been missed by plant breeders. They have developed all kinds of great-tasting varieties for us to enjoy, such as 'Silver Queen', 'Silver King', and 'Peaches and Cream'. This recipe is slightly modified from Aunt Antha's and takes the love of corn to new heights.

SERVES 6 TO 8

4 to 6 ears fresh sweet corn

4 eggs, beaten

2 cups half-and-half

2 tablespoons chopped fresh chives

1 tablespoon cornstarch

1 teaspoon salt

½ teaspoon ground white pepper

4 tablespoons (½ stick) butter, melted

Shuck the corn, and remove the silk. Steam the corn for about 10 minutes, until crisp-tender.

Meanwhile, preheat the oven to 350°F. Generously butter an 8-inch square baking dish, and set it aside.

Standing an ear of corn vertically on a cutting board and using a sharp knife, slice off the kernels, cutting from top to bottom. You should have 3 cups of kernels. Put 2 cups of the kernels in a food processor, and process until finely chopped (this will give the corn pudding a creamier texture).

Stir the eggs and the half-and-half together in a bowl. Add the 2 cups of chopped corn, with its liquid, the remaining 1 cup of whole kernels, and the chives, cornstarch, salt, white pepper, and melted butter. Stir well. Pour this mixture into the baking dish, and bake until the center jiggles just slightly when shaken and the top has begun to turn brown, 30 to 40 minutes. Serve hot.

OKRA FRITTERS

SERVES 4

SERVES 4

Vegetable oil, for frying

2 cups chopped okra

½ onion, chopped

1 teaspoon salt

½ teaspoon freshly
ground black pepper

2 tablespoons all-
purpose flour

⅓ cup yellow or white
cornmeal

2 eggs, beaten

OKRA IS CERTAINLY A SOUTHERN FAVORITE. Over the years it has been fun introducing my Northern friends to the delightful qualities of okra. And while it's not a vegetable found in great abundance above the Mason-Dixon line, I have found it at farmers' markets in Manhattan.

Okra originated in West Africa and was brought to this country in the eighteenth century. The first mention of it as an ingredient in recipes is found in Mary Randolph's famous 1824 cookbook, *The Virginia Housewife,* so by then it was enjoying wide appeal.

Over the years, okra has been prepared in many ways. Because it exudes a clear sticky substance when the pod is cut, it is commonly used as a thickening agent in soups and stews. However, okra can also be steamed, boiled, pickled, sautéed, or stir-fried whole. I like it boiled and cooked with tomatoes. I'm telling you, fixed this way it is the nectar of the garden gods! The secret Southerners often share is that a tablespoon of vinegar added to stews containing okra will neutralize its viscous quality.

These fritters, like fried okra, are delicious with a fresh tomato salad and a dish of field peas (page 110). Yum! And just in case you want to try fried okra, I've slipped that recipe in as well.

Fill a nonreactive skillet (see Note) with ¼ inch of vegetable oil, and heat it over medium-high heat.

Stir the okra and all the remaining ingredients together in a large bowl. Carefully place tablespoonsful of the batter in the hot oil, flattening them slightly with the back of the spoon. Cook until the fritters are golden brown, 1 to 2 minutes per side. As the fritters are done, transfer them to a paper-towel-lined plate to drain. Serve warm.

NOTE: Okra is a sensitive vegetable and should not be cooked in pans made of iron, copper, or brass because their chemical properties turn the okra black.

FRIED OKRA

SERVES 4

Vegetable oil, for frying
½ cup buttermilk
1 egg, beaten

1½ cups white or yellow
   cornmeal
1 cup all-purpose flour

1 teaspoon salt
1 pound okra pods
   (1½ to 2 inches long),
   stems removed

Fill a heavy skillet with 1 to 2 inches of vegetable oil, and heat it over medium-high heat.

Mix the buttermilk and egg together in a small bowl. Combine the cornmeal, flour, and salt in another bowl. One at a time, dip the okra pods in the buttermilk mixture and then roll them in the cornmeal mixture.

Deep-fry the okra pods in the hot oil, a few at a time, until they are crispy, 2 to 3 minutes. Drain on paper towels and serve hot.

If you'd like to try your hand at growing okra, here are a few tips. First, remember it comes from West Africa: the plant thrives in the heat, so plant it when the soil temperatures are warm—late spring or early summer. One of my family members swore that the secret to ensuring good germination was to soak the seeds in milk overnight; apparently the lactic acid in the milk helps break down the hard outer coat of the seed. Once planted, okra seeds will produce pods that are ready to harvest in just 53 days.

GREEN BEANS WITH LEMON VINAIGRETTE AND PARMESAN BREADCRUMBS

SERVES 6

½ cup fresh
  breadcrumbs

½ cup plus 2 tablespoons
  extra-virgin olive oil

Salt and freshly ground
  black pepper

½ cup freshly grated
  Parmigiano-Reggiano
  cheese

Finely grated zest of
  1 lemon (preferably a
  Meyer lemon)

¼ cup fresh lemon juice

¼ cup heavy cream

2 pounds fresh green
  beans, trimmed

THERE IS NOTHING LIKE GREEN BEANS fresh from the garden. That fresh bean taste just can't be found in anything canned or frozen. I like them so much that I eat quite a few straight from the vine while I'm gathering them.

This dish comes together in a snap and is a nice alternative to the usual steamed green beans—plus you get the tang of lemon, which I like. Meyer lemons can be grown from trees treated as houseplants during the winter and brought outdoors in the summer. They are less acidic than standard lemons, and their zest and juice have an herbal, even floral, undertone that makes them worth seeking out.

Preheat the oven to 350°F.

In a small bowl, toss the breadcrumbs with the 2 tablespoons olive oil, a pinch of salt, and a few grinds of the pepper mill. Spread the breadcrumbs out on a rimmed baking sheet, and toast in the oven until golden brown, about 10 minutes. Let the mixture cool, and then transfer it to a bowl and stir in the cheese.

In a medium bowl, whisk the lemon zest and juice, cream, ½ teaspoon salt, and ¼ teaspoon pepper together. Slowly whisk in the remaining ½ cup olive oil.

Bring a large pot of salted water to a boil over high heat. Cook the green beans in the boiling water until tender, 4 to 6 minutes. Drain the beans well, and toss them with the vinaigrette. Taste, and adjust the seasoning if necessary. Transfer the beans to a serving platter, sprinkle with the breadcrumbs, and serve.

BACON-THYME BISCUITS WITH ORANGE MARMALADE BUTTER

MY FRIEND REGINA CHARBONEAU IS A GREAT CHEF. I've enjoyed her flair for Southern food for years. Many of these memorable meals have been enjoyed at her home called Twin Oaks, a handsome antebellum house in Natchez, Mississippi. Regina has a talent for creating all kinds of wonderful dishes, and if there were a contest for National Biscuit Queen, she'd be a top contender. As anyone born and raised in the South can tell you, a good homemade biscuit is a key element of Southern tradition and hospitality. Regina uses her love of the region and her creative spirit to develop some amazingly wonderful biscuit recipes. This one is a favorite of mine. The touch of fresh thyme leaves infuses the dough with a subtle and tantalizing flavor.

MAKES ABOUT 30 BISCUITS

8 ounces sliced bacon

5½ cups all-purpose flour

¼ cup baking powder

¼ cup sugar

¼ cup chopped fresh thyme leaves

1½ cups (3 sticks) cold butter, cut into 1-inch cubes

2 cups Bulgarian buttermilk (see box, page 122) or cultured buttermilk

Orange Marmalade Butter (recipe follows)

Preheat the oven to 375°F.

Cut the bacon into ½-inch pieces, and fry them in a skillet over medium heat until cooked but not crisp. Transfer the bacon to a paper-towel-lined plate, and set it aside. In a medium mixing bowl, combine 5 cups of the flour with the baking powder, sugar, and thyme. Using a pastry blender or a fork, cut the butter into the flour mixture until the butter is the size of very small peas. Add the buttermilk and stir just until all the dry ingredients are incorporated (the key to flaky biscuits is to not overmix).

Sprinkle the remaining ½ cup flour on a work surface or pastry cloth, and turn the biscuit dough onto it. Use a rolling pin to roll the dough into a rectangle about ¾ inch thick. Fold the dough in

recipe continues

half, bringing the two short ends together. Turn it a half turn, and roll it out again.

Sprinkle half of the bacon over the lower half of the dough. Repeat the fold. Turn it a half turn, and roll it out again. Repeat the fold, turn, and roll.

Add the rest of the bacon, and turn and roll two more times. On the seventh and final roll, use the pin to roll the dough to a thickness of approximately ¾ inch.

Cut out the biscuits, using a 2-inch round biscuit or cookie cutter. (For the "no-waste" method, cut the biscuits into squares with a serrated knife.) Place the biscuits ½ inch apart on a 10 x 15-inch ungreased baking sheet. Bake for about 20 minutes, or until golden brown. Serve warm, with the Orange Marmalade Butter.

ORANGE MARMALADE BUTTER
MAKES 1¼ CUPS

1 cup (2 sticks) unsalted butter, at room temperature

¼ cup orange marmalade

In a small bowl, use an electric mixer to whip the butter until it is fluffy and smooth. Add the orange marmalade and continue to whip until the marmalade is blended into the butter. Put the Orange Marmalade Butter in a serving bowl, cover, and chill until ready to use. Bring back to room temperature to serve.

BLUE CHEESE AND ONION CORNBREAD

CORNBREAD HAS ALWAYS BEEN A REGULAR PART of meals in my family. Baked to accompany whatever was being served for supper, a plate of cornbread was not only welcomed, but expected. And to this day, there are some very strong opinions about exactly how it should taste. The great divide falls between the two cornmeal camps of sweet and unsweet. I think my grandmother said it best to a friend who was an advocate of sweet cornbread: "Listen, Lois, you've got to decide if you want cornbread or cake!" I'm squarely in the unsweet camp. And there are other qualities I look for before I can call it "just right": it should be moist on the inside and crisp on the outside. I remember my great-grandmother admonishing one of her six girls about making sure the pork fat in the skillet was so hot that when the batter was poured into it, it crackled and popped. That was the only proper way to ensure a crispy crust, don't you know.

This cornbread is delicious, particularly if you love the flavor of blue cheese—which I adore. Between the eggs and the cheese, this cornbread is plenty moist and loaded with flavor. Just make sure you get the crust right.

The beauty of this approach is that you can dress it up or down. I like to eat this in the simplest way, with a bowl of field peas and green onions (see page 110). But it can take on a more sophisticated air if it is served as small muffins with beef tenderloin or pork chops.

SERVES 8 TO 12

1 Vidalia or other sweet onion, chopped
Pinch of salt
Pinch of freshly ground black pepper (optional)
1½ cups white cornmeal
½ cup all-purpose flour
2 teaspoons baking powder
1 teaspoon baking soda
1½ teaspoons salt
¼ teaspoon cayenne pepper
1½ cups Bulgarian buttermilk (see box, page 122) or cultured buttermilk
2 eggs
4 tablespoons (½ stick) butter, melted
1 cup crumbled blue cheese
3 tablespoons olive oil
1 slice of bacon

Place a cast-iron skillet in the oven and preheat the oven to 425°F. Heat the oil in a heavy skillet over medium-high heat, and add the onions. Add the salt. (The salt will season the onions and speed up the caramelizing process by extracting moisture from the onions, which will eventually evaporate. Be cautious not to add too much salt.) If you like, add a pinch of ground black pepper, too. Cook, stirring the onions. After a minute or so, they may begin to stick to the bottom of the skillet and turn dark in color, which is what should happen. Continue stirring. If it seems the onions

recipe continues

are sticking too much, add a very small amount of water, broth, or wine to the skillet and stir vigorously (this is called "deglazing"—the water will evaporate almost immediately while loosening the onion slices). Continue this process of cooking and deglazing until the onions are deep golden, 25 to 30 minutes. Set them aside.

In a large mixing bowl, combine the cornmeal, flour, baking powder, baking soda, salt, and cayenne pepper.

In a separate bowl, whisk together the buttermilk, eggs, and butter. Mix the wet ingredients into the dry, stirring until well combined. Fold in the blue cheese.

Fry or microwave the slice of bacon, and collect the drippings.

Carefully remove the hot cast-iron skillet from the oven, and add 1 tablespoon of the bacon drippings to it. Swirl the drippings to coat halfway up the sides of the skillet. Place the skillet on top of the stove, and pour the batter into it.

Position the oven rack in the top half of the oven, place the skillet on the rack, and bake for 20 minutes, or until the center is firm to the touch and the top is golden. Remove from the oven, let cool slightly, and cut into wedges.

Cultured Buttermilk vs. Bulgarian Buttermilk

Cultured buttermilk is made by fermenting nonfat or low-fat milk with lactic acid bacteria. In Bulgarian buttermilk, the cream cultures are supplemented or replaced by yogurt cultures and fermented at higher temperatures for higher acidity; it can be more tart and thicker than cultured buttermilk.

HEAVENLY HUSH PUPPIES

I FIND THE HISTORY OF FOOD to be fascinating, so I knew there must be a good story about how hush puppies came by their name. The story I found attributes the origin of this yummy finger food to the settlement of Nouvelle Orléans (later called New Orleans) in the early 1700s. A group of Ursuline nuns, who had come to New Orleans from France, used cornmeal to make a delicious food that they named *croquettes de maise*. The making of these croquettes spread rapidly through the South. Many stories abound about the lore behind the name "hush puppies," but the one I like the most is that an African cook in Atlanta was frying a batch of catfish and croquettes when a nearby puppy began to howl. To keep the young dog quiet, she gave it a plateful of the croquettes and said, "Hush, puppy." Once the name was used, it stuck. Knowing both stories, it only seemed right to call this recipe Heavenly Hush Puppies.

I like the extra bite the jalapeño peppers give these dumplings, and frying them in peanut oil lends a nice rich flavor. I think you'll find that even if your puppy whines, you won't be inclined to share.

MAKES 35 HUSH PUPPIES

6 cups peanut or vegetable oil
1½ cups self-rising cornmeal
½ cup self-rising flour
½ teaspoon baking soda
½ teaspoon salt
1 small onion, chopped
1 tablespoon finely chopped jalapeño pepper
1 cup buttermilk
1 egg, lightly beaten

Heat the oil in a Dutch oven or deep pot, to 350°F. While the oil is heating, stir the cornmeal, flour, baking soda, and salt together. Then mix in the onions and jalapeño pepper.

In a small bowl, stir together the buttermilk and egg. Pour the buttermilk mixture into the dry ingredients, and mix until blended.

Drop the batter, 1 tablespoon at a time, into the hot oil. (Dip the spoon in a glass of water after each hush puppy is dropped in the oil to prevent the batter from sticking.) Fry, turning the hush puppies, until they are golden brown, 2 to 3 minutes. Drain on paper towels and serve warm.

AUNT GENNY'S ZUCCHINI NUT BREAD

SERVES 12 TO 16

2 cups grated unpeeled
  zucchini

2 cups sugar

1 cup vegetable oil

3 eggs, lightly beaten

2 teaspoons vanilla
  extract

3 cups all-purpose flour

1 teaspoon baking soda

1 teaspoon salt

½ teaspoon ground
  cinnamon

1 cup chopped pecans

Grated zest of 1 lemon

AUNT GENNY SHARED THIS RECIPE with my mom years ago, and it has stood the test of time. This zucchini bread has all the qualities I like in a quick bread: it is easy to make, uses up my almost-too-large zucchini, is moist and delicious, and is perfect to put away in the freezer for the cold months ahead. I like the flavor of this bread for a number of reasons: first, it's not too sweet; second, the nuts add a bit of crunch, and as I've mentioned before, I really like a distinctive texture in my food. Which brings me to number three: when this bread is baked in a loaf pan, it slices beautifully and you get four sides of the delectable crust.

I like to cut off a sizable portion, toast it, and then slather it with butter or cream cheese. When I taste it that way, it reminds me of something my dad used to say when he was enjoying something particularly tasty: "I wish I was a giraffe with a neck a mile long and taste buds at every joint!" It is perfect as a breakfast or brunch bread, and a delicious companion to any fruit or chicken salad.

Preheat the oven to 350°F. Generously butter two standard loaf pans, and set them aside.

Place the grated zucchini in a colander and let it drain for 20 minutes. Press on the zucchini to extract the excess moisture. In a large bowl, combine the drained zucchini with the sugar, oil, eggs, and vanilla.

In a medium bowl, combine the flour, baking soda, salt, and cinnamon. Add the dry mixture to the ingredients in the large bowl. Stir in the nuts and the lemon zest.

Divide the batter between the two loaf pans, and bake for 55 minutes. Let the loaves cool in the pans for 10 minutes, and then turn them out onto a wire rack to cool completely.

This bread can also be baked in well-greased muffin tins. Fill each cup three-quarters full of batter, and bake for 35 to 45 minutes. Let cool for 10 minutes, and then turn out onto a wire rack to cool completely.

If you freeze this, I suggest wrapping it in foil after it has completely cooled on a metal rack, then placing it in double freezer bags marked with the contents and date. It is best eaten within 6 months of freezing.

RUSTIC BLACKBERRY COBBLER IN RAMEKINS

I'VE DISCOVERED THAT WHEN I TELL FRIENDS that I'm baking a fruit cobbler for dessert, it means different things to different people. There seem to be two basic camps: the pie crust people and the biscuit dough eaters. While it's not very common, you can sometimes find both camps under the same roof. Typically, once you're raised eating cobblers one way, you rarely stray. To move from one camp to another is like being raised a missionary Baptist and becoming an Episcopalian, which actually happened to me. This can create tense, if not fractious, moments in a family. Now, even though I prefer a pie crust on my cobbler, I must admit that I can still enjoy a cobbler made with biscuit dough.

So, now that I've revealed my preference, it should not surprise you that this recipe calls for a pie crust. And hang on to your hat because I go even further, elevating the humble cobbler with orange zest and Triple Sec. I also like using ramekins because after dishing up two servings, a typical cobbler looks like a train wreck. The ramekins also help to maintain just the right crust-to-juice-to-fruit ratio.

SERVES 8

Butter or flour-based baking spray (such as Baker's Joy)

1 package refrigerated ready-made pie crust (2 crusts), such as Pillsbury

4 cups fresh blackberries (or frozen, if fresh are not available)

½ to 1 cup sugar (to taste), plus more for sprinkling

Salt, to taste

Grated zest of 1 orange

8 teaspoons Triple Sec or fresh orange juice

Melted butter or vegetable cooking spray, for glazing the tops

Heavy cream, sweetened whipped cream, or vanilla ice cream, for serving

recipe continues

reheat the oven to 350°F.

Butter eight 5-ounce ramekins (or spray them with Baker's Joy). Divide each pie crust into quarters. Gently shape and stretch each piece of crust, and then press the crusts into the bottom and up the sides of each ramekin, leaving the uneven edges hanging over the sides.

Mound ½ cup of the blackberries into each crust-lined ramekin. Sprinkle each with 1½ to 2 tablespoons sugar, a pinch of salt, ½ teaspoon orange zest, and 1 teaspoon Triple Sec or orange juice.

Bring the overhanging edges of the pie crust up and over the top of the berries, arranging them loosely. Do not seal. Brush the pastry with melted butter (or spray it lightly with cooking spray) and sprinkle with granulated sugar. Place the ramekins on a baking sheet, and bake for 35 to 45 minutes, or until golden brown and bubbly. Serve warm or at room temperature with cream, sweetened whipped cream, or vanilla ice cream.

LEMON MERINGUE PIE

SERVES 8

FOR THE LEMON FILLING

1¼ cups sugar

2 tablespoons finely grated lemon zest

1 cup fresh lemon juice (from about 6 lemons)

½ cup water

3 tablespoons cornstarch

½ teaspoon salt

8 large egg yolks, at room temperature

4 tablespoons (½ stick) unsalted butter, cut into 4 pieces, at room temperature

FOR THE CRUST

1 Easy Pie Crust, baked (recipe follows)

FOR THE MERINGUE

4 large egg whites

½ teaspoon cream of tartar

½ teaspoon vanilla extract

½ cup sugar

IT'S FUNNY WHAT WE REMEMBER and what we forget from our childhoods. For me, food memories tend to rise to the top. When I was a kid my whole family enjoyed listening to a local radio station called WAKI in McMinnville, Tennessee. They had an early morning show called "Shop and Swap." While we were getting ready for school, an announcer would read off what people had to sell or trade. This was a very popular show because you never knew when you might need a new hay rake or a Jersey heifer.

During the show they would announce what was for lunch at Gaylo Cafeteria, a popular eatery in town. Everyone loved to eat at Gaylo's because they had great home-cooked food, especially their pies. On special occasions Dad would take me with him to eat there. They served meat loaf, mashed potatoes, macaroni and cheese, and chicken-fried steak; you get the idea. And then there were the pies. My favorite was the Mile-High Meringue Pies, so named for their four-inch-high clouds of sweet fluff that covered the filling. I called them "big hairdo pies" because the meringue looked like the big poufy hair styles many of the ladies wore: stacked and sprayed dos that were so popular during the early seventies. Looking back, it seems the higher their hair, the taller the meringue! Under those meringues were different kinds of creamy fillings: chocolate, coconut cream, and lemon. I always chose lemon. This recipe is an attempt to recapture that wonderful childhood memory. Of course nothing today can even compare to those reminiscences from the past, but this one comes close.

I'm also including a pie crust recipe that can be used for any of my recipes calling for a basic crust. Many families have a favored pie crust recipe, and my family is no exception. Most of my relatives take the position that their little crow is the blackest. In my opinion, the pie crust has to meet high standards of flavor, flakiness, and texture, as well as ease of preparation. So for all the reasons above, I think my little crow is the blackest. Give it a try and see what you think. (But if you don't have the time, pick up a prepared crust from the grocery—don't deny yourself a great dessert just because you don't want to make a crust!)

To prepare the filling, whisk the sugar, lemon zest and juice, water, cornstarch, and salt together in a large nonreactive saucepan until the cornstarch has dissolved. Bring the mixture to a simmer over medium heat and cook, whisking occasionally, until it becomes translucent and begins to thicken, about 5 minutes.

Whisk in the egg yolks until combined. Stir in the butter. Bring the mixture to a simmer and stir constantly until it is thick enough to coat the back of a spoon, about 2 minutes.

Strain the filling through a fine-mesh strainer into the baked pie shell, scraping the underside of the strainer to get all the filling. Place a sheet of plastic wrap directly on the surface of the filling, and refrigerate the pie until it is set and well chilled, at least 2 hours and up to 1 day.

Preheat the oven to 375°F.

To prepare the meringue, beat the egg whites with the cream of tartar and vanilla, using an electric mixer on high speed, until soft peaks form. Very slowly add the sugar, continuing to beat until the whites form stiff, glossy peaks and all the sugar has dissolved. Spread the meringue over the lemon filling while the filling is still hot, sealing the meringue to the edge of the pastry. Bake for 12 to 15 minutes, or until the peaks of the meringue are golden. Cool and refrigerate. Before cutting the pie, dip your knife in water to keep the blade from sticking to the meringue.

EASY PIE CRUST

MAKES TWO 9-INCH CRUSTS

2¼ cups all-purpose flour
1 teaspoon salt

⅔ cup vegetable or
canola oil

⅓ cup cold milk

In a bowl, mix the flour and salt together. Measure the oil and milk in the same liquid measuring cup, and add the mixture all at once to the flour mixture. Stir with a spoon until the liquid has been absorbed and the dough forms a ball.

Divide the dough in half. Dampen the countertop with a clean wet cloth, and place a sheet of wax paper over the damp spot. Place one portion of the dough on the wax paper. Place another sheet of wax paper over the dough, and roll it out to the desired thickness for 1 crust.

Remove the top sheet of wax paper. Pick up the bottom sheet, and invert it carefully over a pie plate. Remove the wax paper carefully, working from the edge toward the center. Carefully ease the dough into the pie plate. (Repeat this process for the second crust, or freeze the dough for a later use.)

Preheat the oven to 425°F.

Fold under the edges of the dough to be even with the pie plate and crimp or press with a fork. Prick the bottom and sides of the dough with a fork to prevent bubbles. Bake for 10 to 15 minutes, until the crust is slightly browned.

VARIATION

For a pudding-filled pie or just to give your crust a slightly sweet taste, add 1 tablespoon sugar to the dry ingredients and ½ teaspoon vanilla extract to the liquids, and then prepare the dough as described above.

PEACH MOON TART

STARGAZING IS AN ACTIVITY EVERYONE LOVES at the farm. Well away from city lights, the stars can be viewed with clarity and enjoyed with awe. Watching the full moon rise is great fun, particularly in the summer. This time of year, I often serve dessert and coffee on the front porch after supper and watch the moon as it ascends into the night sky. The view from the east end of the porch is sublime. By July's full moon, the freestone peaches are ripe, and this pie makes good use of them. 'Red Havens' and 'Elbertas' are usually available at the farmers' market. Their color looks like the moon just as it rises above the horizon, going from reddish orange (visible at the core of the peach near the stone) to a rich golden color. If it is a cool evening, I can usually collect enough fresh raspberries ('Dorman Red' or 'Heritage') from the garden to sprinkle among the peaches. These make little "craters" of flavor among the peaches and custard.

Preheat the oven to 350°F.

To make the crust, mix all the ingredients together in a mixing bowl. Press the mixture onto the bottom and up the sides of a 9½-inch fluted-edge tart pan with removable bottom. Place the tart pan on a baking sheet, and bake in the center of the oven for 10 minutes. Allow the crust to cool completely in the pan before filling it.

While the crust is cooling, place the peach wedges in a bowl and pour the peach brandy over them; set aside.

Once the crust is cool, remove the peaches from the brandy with a slotted spoon, reserving the liquid, and arrange the wedges in circles on the tart crust. Scatter the raspberries on top of the peaches.

In a mixing bowl, combine the eggs, cream, sugar, nutmeg, and the reserved peach brandy. Pour the mixture over the fruit in the tart pan.

Place the tart pan on a baking sheet and bake for 35 to 45 minutes, or until the custard is set and lightly browned. Let the pie cool to room temperature, and then cut it into slices to serve.

SERVES 8

FOR THE CRUST

1½ cups slivered almonds, lightly toasted and ground

1½ cups gingersnap cookie crumbs (grind the cookies in a blender or processor)

¼ cup sugar

6 tablespoons (¾ stick) butter, melted

½ teaspoon almond extract

FOR THE FILLING

4 to 6 fresh, ripe peaches, peeled and sliced into wedges

⅓ cup peach brandy

1 cup fresh raspberries

4 large eggs, lightly beaten

1½ cups heavy cream

¾ cup sugar

½ teaspoon freshly grated nutmeg

POMEGRANATE MERLOT SORBET

SERVES 6

3 cups bottled
 pomegranate juice
¼ cup fresh lemon juice
1 cup water
1 cup merlot wine
1 cup sugar

YEARS AGO I DISCOVERED what struck me as a sensual marriage between two of my favorite flavors: merlot wine and pomegranate juice. I discovered this elixir in a small shop in California. I bought one bottle to give it a try. Soon I was pouring it over everything from pork to sorbet, so I ordered more, used that, ordered more, used that, and then it finally occurred to me to ask one of my favorite local stores to keep it in stock. That arrangement made for a convenient and reliable source until the owners told me that they were no longer able to get it and that, quite sadly, the small family enterprise that had been producing it had closed its doors. Far too often this is the case for such things.

Not to be outdone, I embarked on creating my own recipe, trying various proportions of merlot to pomegranate juice. I tinkered with the quality of the wine (the worst is as good as the best, I discovered) and the source of the pomegranate juice (no need to squeeze your own, I assure you), and of course various methods of making the reduction itself. What I discovered is that it's easy, quick, and delicious, and should you begin your own enterprise to produce this product commercially, please let me know.

This recipe takes the basic merlot/pomegranate duo and turns it into a wonderful sorbet. See if you aren't as captivated as I am with this combination.

Combine all the ingredients in a medium nonreactive saucepan, and bring to a boil over medium-high heat. Continue to boil the mixture for approximately 45 minutes, reducing it by about half to a syrup consistency. Remove the syrup from the heat and let it cool to room temperature.

Transfer the syrup to an ice cream maker, and process according to the manufacturer's directions.

Transfer the sorbet to an airtight container and store it in the freezer. Remove the sorbet from the freezer and let it stand for 10 minutes before serving.

FALL

PEPPERED WALNUTS

I AM A BLACK PEPPER FIEND, so I tend to use a heavy hand when it comes to adding this wonderful spice to dishes. It's hard to hold back because I love it so much, and I add it to nearly everything.

The combination of black pepper and walnuts in this recipe creates an appetizer with a lovely fall flavor. Nutty foods are popular around the holidays, but they often take the form of sweets. I like this rendition because of its savory blend.

Now don't wait until company is knocking on your door to start preparing these—they are a great make-ahead treat. Toast up a bunch, enjoy some yourself, and then slide the rest into an airtight container and store them in the freezer for several months, if you don't eat them all right away. Then when guests come by, heat them up and serve them with a glass of red wine while sitting around a crackling fire.

MAKES 4 CUPS

4 cups walnut halves
⅔ cup sugar
1 teaspoon salt
1 tablespoon cracked
   black pepper

Combine the walnuts and sugar in a nonstick skillet, and cook over medium heat, stirring with a wooden spoon, until the sugar begins to dissolve. Keep stirring while adding the salt and pepper.

After the sugar has melted and the walnuts are well coated, pour them onto a sheet of wax paper. Separate the walnuts as much as possible with the wooden spoon, and allow them to cool completely.

Store the walnuts in an airtight container at room temperature until you are ready to serve them. These will keep for weeks at room temperature and for several months in the freezer.

APPLETINI

SERVES 2

2 ounces (¼ cup) vodka

6 ounces (¾ cup) applejack or Calvados (French apple brandy)

Juice of 1 lemon

2 teaspoons superfine sugar

2 apple slices, for garnish

2 maraschino cherries, for garnish

TO CELEBRATE THE FALL APPLE HARVEST, I enjoy serving this appletini. It is a fun way to kick off a party—think of it as bobbing for apples in a martini glass. The key to the presentation is using a small apple that is proportional in size to the martini glass. Lady apples are ideal if you can find them. They are another heritage variety, with a beautiful blend of green and red outer skin and white, firm flesh with a tangy flavor.

Pour the vodka, applejack, lemon juice, and sugar into a cocktail shaker, and shake with ice. Strain the mixture into two chilled martini glasses. Garnish each one with an apple slice and a maraschino cherry, and serve.

The apple has been long described as Nature's most pleasure-laden food, with epic stories associating the fruit with love, beauty, health, wisdom, temptation, and fertility. Few other foods have such a legendary status—all the way back to the Garden of Eden! In 1872, there were 1,100 uniquely American apple varieties in the United States. Today only a few varieties are available in most supermarkets. To enjoy the special flavor of the apples that date back to those early days, orchards are now specializing in growing heirloom varieties in an attempt to preserve America's apple heritage. I've joined the cause and grow seventeen varieties of apples at the Garden Home Retreat. The oldest heritage variety is Calville Blanc d'Hiver, a French apple that dates back to the 1500s; it was grown in Louis XIII's gardens at Orléans and by Thomas Jefferson at Monticello. It's fun to know that these wonderful fruits with such long histories are still being grown and appreciated.

OREGANO AND GARLIC MARINATED GRILLED SHRIMP

SERVES 4 TO 6

8 6-inch wooden skewers, soaked in water for 1 hour (optional)

16 extra-large shrimp, tails on, shelled and deveined

½ cup olive oil

3 garlic cloves, coarsely chopped

2 tablespoons chopped fresh oregano leaves

2 tablespoons chopped fresh flat-leaf parsley leaves

½ teaspoon red pepper flakes

1 teaspoon salt

KIDS AREN'T ALWAYS THE MOST ADVENTUROUS EATERS, but I've found that if I can get them interested in what I'm preparing, they will be engaged enough to give it a taste. One activity that's fun is to trace the meanings of the names of the ingredients in a recipe. For instance, the word *shrimp* comes from the Middle English *shrimpe*, meaning "pygmy," referring to the size of the crustacean. *Oregano* means "joy of the mountain," from the Greek *oros*. *Garlic* comes from the Old English *garleac*, meaning "spear leek." So there you have it: Pygmy Crustacean marinated with Joy of the Mountain and Spear Leek. It's a fun name that will bring young and old to the table.

Among adults, my experience is that no matter what you call them, these shrimp go so fast that you may want to double the recipe. To make the presentation even more interesting, serve the shrimp on skewers with olives and cubes of feta cheese.

In a medium bowl, combine the shrimp with all the other ingredients. Let the shrimp marinate in the mixture for 1 hour at room temperature.

Preheat a barbecue grill to medium (see Note).

Remove the shrimp from the marinade, thread each skewer with 2 shrimp, and grill them for 2 to 3 minutes on each side, or until they turn pink and are cooked through. Place on a platter to serve.

NOTE: These shrimp may also be cooked in a grill basket outdoors, or indoors on a grill pan.

PARMESAN PECAN CRISPS

LIVING IN THE HEART OF PECAN COUNTRY has its perks. When the nut harvest begins in October, I like to buy several bags at a roadside stand so I'll have plenty on hand for preparing some of my favorite pecan treats, such as pecan rolls, sandies, nut muffins, pecan stuffed eggs, pecan clusters, and of course pecan pie. This recipe adds one more to the list of the many ways to enjoy pecans. It pairs Parmesan cheese with pecans for crispy little nibbles that are always a big hit at gatherings.

SERVES 4

1 cup freshly grated Parmesan cheese

2 tablespoons finely chopped pecans

½ teaspoon cracked black peppercorns

Preheat the oven to 350°F. Line a baking sheet with a silicone baking mat or parchment paper.

Mix the grated Parmesan with the chopped pecans and pepper, and using a tablespoon, put little round heaps of the mixture on the baking sheet. Press the heaps down with the back of a wooden spoon or with your fingers, and bake for 7 to 8 minutes, until the crisps just begin to color.

Remove the baking sheet from the oven and allow the crisps to cool a little before using a small metal spatula to transfer them to a wire rack. As they cool, they will crisp up and be less likely to break.

Serve at room temperature. These crisps will keep for a couple of weeks in an airtight container.

For fresh and flavorful nuts, choose whole pecans in the shell that are heavy for their size and don't rattle when shaken. Avoid those with cracks or holes in the shells. Unshelled, the pecans can be stored for about 3 months at room temperature. If you buy shelled pecans in bags or cans, look for the expiration date: the fresher the better. Shelled pecans absorb odors and turn rancid quickly, so be sure to store them in a sealed container in the refrigerator. Pecans also freeze very well, so if you buy more than you can use right away, put them in a moisture-proof plastic bag or other airtight container and store them in the freezer.

ROASTED RED PEPPER SOUP

I AM OF THE OPINION that the red bell pepper is its most exquisite when roasted. There is something about the way the sugars condense and caramelize on the open grill that makes them taste completely different than the raw version.

Prepared just as it is, this soup is smooth, rich, and wholly satisfying. But sometimes I'll top it with a dollop of sour cream just before serving; or I might stir in some chopped tomatoes while it is simmering on the stove.

Preheat the broiler to high.

Cut the bell peppers in half, and remove the seeds and ribs. Lay the peppers, skin side up, on a baking sheet and drizzle them with olive oil; then season them with 1½ teaspoons salt and ½ teaspoon pepper. Broil for 15 to 20 minutes, or until the peppers are charred.

Carefully remove the peppers from the oven. Place them in a glass bowl, cover it tightly with plastic wrap, and let the peppers steam for about 20 minutes. (This will allow the skin to peel off the pepper flesh easily.) Once the peppers are cool, peel off the charred skin. Set the roasted peppers aside.

Preheat the oven to 350°F.

Cut the tomatoes in half, and roughly chop the onion, garlic, and chile. Put the vegetables in a baking pan. In a small bowl, mix the vinegar and oil together; pour this over the vegetables, making sure everything is well coated. Roast the vegetables in the oven, turning them from time to time, for 45 minutes.

Transfer the roasted vegetables to a food processor. Add the red peppers and some of the broth, and pulse until pureed. Thin the soup to the consistency you want with the remaining broth, and season it with salt and pepper to taste. If you will be serving it immediately, warm the soup for a few minutes in a saucepan. Or put it in the fridge to cool before reheating and serving later.

To serve, add a dollop of sour cream, if desired, and some chopped basil leaves.

SERVES 6

3 to 4 red bell peppers (about 1½ pounds)

3 tablespoons extra-virgin olive oil, plus extra for drizzling on the peppers

Salt and freshly ground black pepper

1½ pounds ripe tomatoes, or 2 cups canned diced tomatoes with their juice

1 red onion

3 garlic cloves

½ dried red chile

1 tablespoon balsamic vinegar

4 cups good chicken or vegetable broth

Sour cream (optional)

Fresh basil leaves, chopped

AFTER-THANKSGIVING TURKEY SANDWICH WITH CRANBERRY CHUTNEY

SERVES 6

12 slices sourdough
   bread, or
   6 sourdough rolls

Cranberry Chutney
   (recipe follows)

Leftover Thanksgiving
   heritage turkey, sliced

4 ounces aged Brie,
   thinly sliced

1 to 2 cups fresh
   arugula, rinsed
   thoroughly and
   patted dry

12 slices bacon, cooked
   crisp

Butter, at room
   temperature

THANKSGIVING IS A TREASURED HOLIDAY in my house. I usually finish up planting the last of my spring-flowering bulbs about then and am ready to enjoy a big meal. Along with the fun of being with family and friends, it's a celebration of an abundant harvest and all the good food that goes with the season. The table laid out with turkey, cornbread dressing, salads, vegetables, rolls, and pies is a sight to behold. It really is a day to pause and give thanks for the abundance of all we enjoy.

After sampling every dish more than once, I always leave the table vowing I'll never eat again. And then about two hours later, I'm surprised to find myself standing in front of an open refrigerator, staring inside and thinking, "Maybe I could have just a bite or two more." That moment was the inspiration for this sandwich. I think I may enjoy after-Thanksgiving turkey as much as I do the initial roast. It seems to get better as time goes by and is the perfect excuse to invite a few friends to the house the day after the holiday to help "clean up" some of the leftovers.

In fact, this has become a popular after-the-crowd-thins-out event, and this sandwich is always on the menu. Adding some crisp bacon, spicy arugula, Brie, and tangy cranberry chutney to the turkey creates a delicious medley of flavors that I enjoy all over again.

Spread one slice of the bread, or one side of a roll, with cranberry chutney, and top it with sliced turkey. Spread the other slice of bread or the other side of the roll with Brie. Add arugula and two slices of crisp bacon.

Heat an iron skillet or griddle over medium-high heat.

Butter the outside of the bread or rolls, and grill the sandwiches in the skillet or on the griddle until golden brown on both sides. Serve immediately.

recipe continues

CRANBERRY CHUTNEY

MAKES 5 CUPS

3½ cups fresh cranberries, or one 1-pound package frozen cranberries

1 Granny Smith apple, peeled, cored, and finely chopped

2 navel oranges: 1 segmented and 1 juiced

½ cup golden raisins

1 onion, finely chopped

1 cup light brown sugar, packed

¼ teaspoon ground cloves

¼ teaspoon ground ginger

¼ teaspoon ground allspice

¼ teaspoon ground white pepper

½ teaspoon salt

In a large saucepan, combine the cranberries, chopped apple, orange segments and juice, golden raisins, and chopped onion. Add the brown sugar, spices, and salt to the mixture. Bring to a boil over medium heat and cook, stirring often, for about 20 minutes, or until thick and bubbly.

Remove the pan from the heat and allow the chutney to cool completely. Serve right away, and store any leftovers in the refrigerator for up to 2 weeks.

ROSEMARY CANNELLINI SOUP

BEANS AND CORNBREAD, along with some fresh onions and chow-chow (a traditional Southern relish of summer vegetables cooked in a vinegar mixture), were mainstays on the supper table when I was growing up. Apparently that meal was served a little too often for my brother's liking, because one night he announced to everyone that he'd like to have something else besides beans and cornbread. My grandmother, who was visiting at the time, quickly replied that she was sure there was going to be something different on the table for him the next day: for a change, instead of beans and cornbread she'd fix him some nice cornbread and beans. Everyone at the table burst out laughing. Now when we get together, we'll often ask as the dish is served, "Is this the beans and cornbread recipe or cornbread and beans?"

This dish harkens back to that recipe, but with a few significant changes: lovely cannellini beans and rosemary. Heavens, this is good! To accompany the soup, try some Blue Cheese and Onion Cornbread (page 121) along with the Spiced Red Cabbage with Apples and Thyme (page 165).

Drain the beans. Combine half of the beans with the green onions, herbs, salt, pepper, and olive oil in a food processor fitted with the metal blade and puree. Transfer the puree to a large, heavy saucepan, and pour in the vegetable broth.

Mix well and bring to a boil. Reduce the heat and simmer, covered, for 20 minutes.

Stir in the remaining whole beans and simmer for 10 minutes more. Drizzle with a little olive oil, and serve hot.

SERVES 8

- 4 15-ounce cans cannellini beans
- 4 green onions, white and green parts, chopped
- 2 teaspoons finely chopped fresh rosemary leaves
- 2 teaspoons finely chopped fresh thyme leaves
- 1 teaspoon finely chopped fresh oregano leaves
- 1 fresh sage leaf, finely chopped
- ½ teaspoon salt
- ½ teaspoon freshly ground black pepper
- ⅓ cup extra-virgin olive oil, plus extra for drizzling
- 2 cups vegetable broth or water

BLACK AND WHITE GRAPE SALAD

SO OFTEN FOOD DESCRIBED as a "fall recipe" can be heavy with ingredients that include potatoes and other root vegetables. This salad helps counterbalance that fare: it is light and delightful. The combination of dark and light grapes is as pretty on the plate as it is sweet and refreshing to the palate.

SERVES 6 TO 8

1 pound seedless black or red grapes

1 pound seedless green grapes

Grated zest of 1 orange

⅓ cup superfine sugar

6 oranges: 3 segmented, 3 juiced (or more if needed)

1 cup crumbled goat cheese

½ cup roasted salted walnuts or pecans

Detach all the grapes from their stems. Cut the black or red grapes in half around the middle. If the green grapes are small, leave them whole; if not, slice them in half lengthwise. Put the grapes in a bowl, and add the orange zest and the sugar. Next, add the orange segments and mix gently.

Add the orange juice. There should be just enough liquid to cover the fruit; if not, add a little more juice. Mix thoroughly, cover, and chill for at least 2 hours.

When you are ready to serve the salad, use a slotted spoon to transfer the grapes and oranges to individual salad plates. Top each serving with about 2 tablespoons of the goat cheese and 1 tablespoon of the nuts.

A grapevine-covered arbor is a beautiful addition to your outdoor entertaining space, and the great American muscadine is ideal for this project. Choose 'Black Beauty' for large purple fruits or 'Scuppernong' for medium-size bronze fruits. Install the arbor at the same time you plant—even though grapes may not need the support until their second year, establishing the arbor and plants together will ensure the roots aren't disturbed later and will also make training the vines easier.

CURLY ENDIVE
WITH DATES
AND WALNUTS

SERVES 6

2 shallots, finely
  chopped

2 tablespoons balsamic
  vinegar

¾ cup walnuts

2 heads (about 1 pound)
  curly endive

12 pitted dates (figs can
  be substituted when
  in season)

½ cup olive oil

Salt and freshly ground
  black pepper

ENDIVE IS A COOL-WEATHER GREEN valued for its distinct clean, sharp taste in the salad bowl. You'll find it in the grocery store, but it's a bit expensive, so I grow it in the garden to save money and get the best quality. Endive doesn't like hot weather, and in fact it can take some pretty hard frosts, so it is a good fall-to-winter green at the Garden Home Retreat. We use frost blankets over the greens to bring them through the coldest nights.

There are many cultivars of endive. I used 'Salad King' for this recipe. There is also the endive known as escarole, or broad chicory, that is a less curly form with broader leaves. And, of course, the broadest leaf of all is Belgian endive.

To pick out curly endive in the store, look for tightly furled, crisp leaves that have a fresh look. Avoid those with lots of discoloration—that's an indication that the greens were not handled well.

This salad sets up an interesting interplay of contrasting flavors and textures. I find the combination of the tangy endive with sweet dates and crunchy walnuts to be just delightful.

Place the shallots in a small bowl, and add the vinegar. Set aside to marinate for about 20 minutes.

Meanwhile, preheat the oven to 350°F. Spread the walnuts on a baking sheet and toast them in the oven for 5 to 8 minutes, until crisp and fragrant.

Tear off the tough outer leaves of the curly endive, saving only the pale green and white tender hearts (reserve the outer leaves for cooking greens). Cut out the core and plunge the leaves into a sink filled with cold water. Gently agitate the greens and let them soak for a few minutes. Then remove the leaves and dry them thoroughly.

Chop 6 of the dates very fine, and add them to the shallots. Whisk in the olive oil, and season with salt and pepper to taste.

Just before serving, quarter the remaining 6 dates and toss them in a large bowl with the endive, walnuts, and just enough dressing to coat all the elements. Serve immediately.

CRUNCHY PEAR SALAD

SERVES 6

2 celery ribs

¼ cup apple cider, pear, raspberry, or other fruit vinegar

¼ cup honey

¼ teaspoon salt

2 ripe but crisp pears, cored and thinly sliced

6 cups butterhead or other lettuce

¾ cup crumbled blue cheese

¾ cup salted pecans

Freshly ground black pepper

WHEN I WAS A KID, it seemed like every house in our rural community had some kind of fruit tree in the yard. I especially remember the way the pear trees looked in the autumn, when their gnarled branches became weighted down with beautiful fruit. Most of these trees were a tough old variety called 'Keifer'. It's a pear that survives in the South without much care or spraying. My grandmother Kee Kee favored this pear for making pear cake and pear honey, a preserve that in my mind was akin to pure nectar from the pear gods.

I grow 'Keifer' pears in an espaliered candelabra form at the Garden Home Retreat, under the tutelage of my friend Peter Thevenot at River Road Farm in Tennessee. His methods of espalier are inspired by the work of Father Legendre of Hanonsville, France, who is credited with pioneering this type of artistic pruning in the 1600s. Peter's passion for this unique art form runs deep and remains true to the spirit and techniques of the European tradition. He has helped me to keep the espaliered fruit trees in good order.

Cut the celery into ¼-inch pieces, and soak them in a bowl of ice water for 15 minutes. Drain and pat dry.

Whisk the vinegar, honey, and salt together in a large bowl until blended. Add the pears and celery, and gently stir (or use your clean hands) to coat them with the mixture.

Divide the lettuce leaves among six plates, and using a slotted spoon, top each leaf with a portion of the pears and celery, reserving the vinaigrette. Top each salad with 2 tablespoons of the blue cheese and 2 tablespoons of the pecans. Drizzle the salads with the remaining vinaigrette, and season with some freshly ground pepper. Serve at room temperature or chilled.

EGGPLANT AND FETA SALAD

EGGPLANT IS QUITE ABUNDANT IN THE GARDEN at the end of the summer season, and this salad is a good use of this beautiful vegetable. There are many different varieties available, so the benefit of growing your own is that you'll have the eggplants you need for the dish you want to prepare. There are solid purples, purple-and-white streaked, white, green, dwarf, elongated, ribbed, and smooth varieties, so take your pick. The difference in appearance comes from the eggplant's wide-ranging origins, with different varieties hailing from all over the globe, including Africa, Italy, Thailand, India, China, and the Ukraine.

Preheat the oven to 425°F.

In a small bowl, whisk together the olive oil, lemon juice, salt, and pepper to make a vinaigrette. In a large bowl, toss the eggplant with ⅓ cup of the dressing, reserving the rest.

Arrange the eggplant in a single layer on a baking sheet. Bake, tossing the chunks occasionally, until they are tender and golden around the edges, about 30 minutes. Let the eggplant cool somewhat. (It can be warm, but it should not be hot enough to melt the feta or wilt the mint.)

Gently fold the feta, garlic, capers, tomatoes, and mint into the reserved vinaigrette, being careful not to "muddy" the vinaigrette by mashing the feta. Arrange the eggplant on a platter, and spoon the feta-tomato mixture evenly over the top. Garnish with whole cherry tomatoes and sprigs of mint, and serve.

SERVES 6

- ½ cup extra-virgin olive oil
- ¼ cup fresh lemon juice
- ¾ teaspoon kosher salt
- ½ teaspoon freshly ground black pepper
- 3 pounds eggplant, peeled and cut into 1-inch chunks
- 3 ounces feta cheese, crumbled (about ⅔ cup)
- 2 garlic cloves, minced
- 2 tablespoons small capers, drained
- 1 cup cherry tomatoes, halved
- ¼ cup fresh mint leaves, finely chopped
- Whole cherry tomatoes and fresh mint sprigs, for garnish

RED PEPPER FRITTATA WITH PROSCIUTTO

MAKING A FRITTATA IS VERY SIMILAR to making a garden: you adapt to what you have on hand and the conditions you have to work with. Some of my best frittata creations have occurred when the fridge was bare and the garden was thin, so I was forced to be inventive with what was on hand.

This frittata is a favorite of mine. It lets me use up many of the end-of-season vegetables, such as red peppers and leeks. It's perfect to serve for breakfast and even better for brunch. It's also a great Sunday night supper with a fresh green salad and a glass of wine. I've even enjoyed it with cheese grits or alongside roasted potatoes!

Above all, the key to making a frittata is to just have fun. Sweep through the garden/pantry/refrigerator and come up with your own version.

SERVES 6 TO 8

4 red bell peppers

3 medium-size potatoes, chopped

3 tablespoons olive oil

2 tablespoons butter

4 ounces sliced prosciutto, cut into strips

2 leeks, white and green parts, sliced in half lengthwise, well rinsed, and cut into thin half-moons

4 garlic cloves, minced

6 eggs

¾ cup heavy cream

Salt and freshly ground black pepper

Freshly grated nutmeg

4 ounces goat cheese

½ cup freshly grated Parmesan cheese

¼ cup chopped fresh chives

Preheat the oven to 400°F.

Lay the peppers on a baking sheet and roast them, turning them as needed, until the skins are well charred all over, about 30 minutes. Then put the peppers in a plastic bag and let them steam for about 20 minutes. Once the peppers are cool enough to handle, peel off the charred skin and cut the roasted peppers into strips. Set the strips aside.

Reduce the oven temperature to 350°F.

Rinse the chopped potatoes under cold running water, drain, and pat dry. Set them aside.

Heat 2 tablespoons of the olive oil and 1 tablespoon of the butter in an ovenproof skillet. When the mixture is foaming, add the prosciutto and leeks, and cook until the prosciutto is crispy and the leeks are translucent, about 10 minutes. Transfer the mixture to a plate and set it aside.

recipe continues

Add 1 more tablespoon each butter and olive oil to the skillet, and cook the potatoes over medium heat until they are tender, about 15 minutes. Stir in the garlic, and remove the skillet from the heat.

In a large bowl, whisk the eggs with the cream. Season with plenty of salt, pepper, and nutmeg. Stir in the cooked leeks and prosciutto, the goat cheese, most of the Parmesan, the chopped chives, and the roasted peppers. Pour this over the potatoes in the skillet, stirring gently to combine. Put the skillet back on the heat and cook for just a couple of minutes, until the bottom of the frittata is beginning to set.

Transfer the skillet to the oven, and cook for 10 minutes, until the frittata is just firm to the touch. Invert the frittata onto a large plate. (I think the top looks nicer, so I suggest flipping it back again.) Then allow it to rest for 5 minutes (it has far less flavor when it's piping hot). Garnish with the remaining Parmesan, cut into wedges, and serve.

I'm often asked how to grow red bell peppers. Believe it or not, green bell peppers and the red peppers are one and the same. Much like a tomato plant, peppers have green immature fruit that develops into red mature fruit. And, just like a tomato, the mature fruit can also be yellow or orange. So for a green pepper to turn into a red pepper, all you need is to give it some time to mature. How much time? It depends on the variety. Most varieties of red peppers need more than 100 days to reach maturity. If you want red peppers sooner, consider planting varieties that will mature in less time, say 65 to 70 days. (For this information, look on the seed packet or plant tag.)

GRILLED TUNA WITH HERB-INFUSED OIL

THE MONTH OF SEPTEMBER is often thought of as the beginning of fall, but where I am in the mid-South, there's still plenty of summer sizzle left, and I can enjoy grilling and entertaining outdoors well into October.

No matter where you live, before you hang up the grill tongs for the season, give this recipe a try: olive oil and fresh herbs enhance the mild flavor of the grilled tuna steak. Served with a little mango chutney, this has become my favorite "fare-well to summer and hello to fall" meal.

There seem to be two schools of thought when grilling tuna: some like to sear it so that the outside is charred but the inside is still very rare, while others prefer it cooked all the way through. I split the difference and grill it until it still has a little pink in the center. The key here is the extra-virgin olive oil; its rich emulsifiers penetrate the fish. The olive oil marinade also helps keep the fish moist on the grill, an advantage with thinner steaks.

SERVES 4

¼ cup extra-virgin olive oil
Grated zest and juice of 1 lemon
Juice of 1 orange
1 tablespoon chopped fresh thyme leaves
1 tablespoon chopped fresh flat-leaf parsley leaves
1 tablespoon chopped fresh oregano leaves
1 tablespoon peeled and finely chopped fresh ginger
2 garlic cloves, minced
1 teaspoon soy sauce
Pinch of red pepper flakes
4 8-ounce tuna steaks
Mango chutney, for serving

Combine all the ingredients except the tuna and the chutney in a saucepan, and warm the mixture gently over low heat until you start to smell the herb and garlic aroma. The key here is not to boil the oil. Remove the saucepan from the heat and let the marinade cool.

Put the tuna steaks in a baking dish or a gallon-size zip-top plastic bag, and pour the marinade over them. Marinate the steaks in the refrigerator for at least 4 hours or up to 1 day.

Grill the tuna steaks for about 6 minutes on each side, or 4 minutes on each side if you prefer pink tuna at the center. (Cook the steaks over medium-high heat on an outdoor gas grill, or 6 inches from hot, prepared charcoal.) Top with mango chutney and serve immediately.

SHRIMP CREOLE

SERVES 8

⅓ cup vegetable oil

⅓ cup all-purpose flour

2 onions, finely
   chopped

2 celery ribs, finely
   chopped

3 garlic cloves, finely
   chopped

1 large green bell
   pepper, finely
   chopped

½ teaspoon cayenne
   pepper

1 teaspoon freshly
   ground black pepper

2½ teaspoons salt

2 tablespoons finely
   chopped fresh flat-
   leaf parsley leaves

1 tablespoon chopped
   fresh thyme leaves, or
   1 teaspoon dried

4 cups finely diced
   tomatoes

2 bay leaves

3 pounds shrimp,
   peeled and deveined

2 tablespoons
   Worcestershire sauce

2 cups rice

I'D BE REMISS IN MY DUTIES as a son of the South if I didn't mention that the essential ingredient in Shrimp Creole is not the shrimp or the spices, but the rice. My home state, Arkansas, is our nation's number-one producer of rice, growing nearly 48 percent of the total crop on more than 1.3 million acres, so the rice you'll buy for this recipe was likely grown in Arkansas.

This recipe for shrimp Creole offers a complex layering of flavors and is delightfully rich with wonderful seasonings. This is a good dish to cook with a group of friends who might come by around noon, hang out in the kitchen to help put this together, and then enjoy eating it later in the afternoon.

I also like to make it ahead and serve it the night before Thanksgiving, when I know there will be friends and family in the house. It's a nice contrast to the holiday meal and an easy serve-yourself food. I make it in a big cast-iron kettle and keep it on the stove, and put out the rice, a green salad, and baguettes. It's become as much a Thanksgiving tradition at my house as the roast turkey.

Begin by making a dark, rich roux: Heat the oil in a heavy Dutch oven over medium-high heat until it just begins to smoke. Whisk in the flour, and continue whisking until the roux is the color of an old penny.

All together, add the onions, celery, garlic, bell peppers, cayenne pepper, black pepper, and salt. Stir over medium-high heat until the onions brown slightly, 4 to 5 minutes. Next, add the parsley, thyme, diced tomatoes, and bay leaves. Finally, add the shrimp. Cover the pot and simmer for 1 hour.

Meanwhile, prepare the rice according to the package directions.

Just before serving, stir the Worcestershire sauce into the shrimp mixture, and adjust the seasonings to taste (see Note). Discard the bay leaf.

Serve the Shrimp Creole over the cooked rice.

NOTE: If you are making the Shrimp Creole ahead of time, remember that flavors get stronger after a day or two in the refrigerator, so don't overdo the last-minute seasoning.

ROASTED CHICKEN WITH DIJON VINAIGRETTE

THE DIJON MUSTARD IN THE VINAIGRETTE gives this recipe a rustic aspect and lends an earthy quality to the dish that brings the roasted chicken to life. Prepared in a cast-iron Dutch oven, it makes a handsome presentation that just feels like autumn. Serve it with the Crunchy Pear Salad (page 152) or the Curly Endive with Dates and Walnuts (page 150).

The difference between Dijon and other mustards has to do with the types and flavor variations. In France there are three types: Dijon, which is fairly light in color but strong in flavor; Bordeaux, a darker, milder, more vinegary mustard; and Meaux, a mild mustard made from crushed seeds.

Preheat the oven to 450°F.

To prepare the vinaigrette, combine the mustard and vinegar in a medium bowl and mix well. Gradually whisk in the olive oil. Then stir in the shallots, rosemary, sage, garlic, salt, and pepper. Set aside.

To prepare the chicken, discard the neck and giblets, rinse the chicken thoroughly inside and out, and pat it dry. Season the cavity with salt and pepper to taste. Place the quartered shallots and the sprigs of rosemary and sage inside the cavity. Lift the breast skin on each side of the chicken, forming 2 pockets, and spread 1 tablespoon of the mustard vinaigrette between the skin and the breast meat on each side. Truss the legs, and tuck the wings under the body of the chicken.

Place the chicken in a roasting pan and brush the entire outer surface with some of the remaining vinaigrette. Sprinkle with the chopped rosemary and sage, and season with salt and pepper to taste.

Roast for 20 minutes. Then reduce the temperature to 375°F and roast, basting the chicken occasionally with any remaining vinaigrette or with the pan juices, for 1 hour and 20 minutes, or until the juices run clear when the thickest part of the thigh is pierced.

Transfer the chicken to a platter, garnish with additional sprigs of rosemary and sage, and serve.

SERVES 4 TO 6

FOR THE DIJON VINAIGRETTE
¼ cup Dijon mustard

¼ cup white wine vinegar

¾ cup olive oil

⅔ cup chopped shallots

2 tablespoons chopped fresh rosemary leaves

1 tablespoon chopped fresh sage leaves

4 garlic cloves, finely chopped

½ teaspoon salt

½ teaspoon coarsely ground black pepper

FOR THE CHICKEN
1 6- to 7-pound heritage roasting chicken

Salt and freshly ground black pepper

2 shallots, cut into quarters

2 fresh rosemary sprigs, plus more for garnish

1 fresh sage sprig, plus more for garnish

1 tablespoon chopped fresh rosemary leaves

1 tablespoon chopped fresh sage leaves

CITRUS-GLAZED TURKEY BREAST

SERVES 8

Grated zest and juice of
1 orange

Grated zest and juice of
1 lime

¼ cup honey

½ teaspoon salt

½ teaspoon freshly
ground black pepper

1 3-pound boneless
heritage turkey
breast, thawed if
frozen

¼ cup olive oil

WHEN I WAS ELEVEN YEARS OLD, I was in the local 4-H Club and entered my chickens in the county fair's poultry show. Along with several ribbons, I won a sizable chunk of change in prize money. Instead of buying games or candy, I purchased my first trio of Bronze turkeys. I had seen those big beautiful birds and knew I had to have them. Since then, I've been hooked on raising various breeds of turkeys, chickens, ducks, and geese. The experience has taught me valuable lessons about the importance of heritage livestock and poultry to the health and economy of our nation's farms.

Sometime in the 1960s most of the poultry raised in this country began moving from small farms to commercial industrial growers. This has increasingly narrowed breeds and genetics to just a few types. That meant that the beautiful heritage breeds no longer had a commercial purpose, and the flock sizes dwindled to near extinction. This has been alarming to small-farm poultry breeders. Without healthy, large flock sizes, the genetics of the remaining birds became poor. In the spirit of that cause, I, along with others, have established the Heritage Poultry Conservancy. The purpose is to encourage more people to raise and sell heritage breeds of poultry and to create markets for this type of egg and meat. This recipe is especially delicious when prepared with a heritage-breed turkey.

Preheat the oven to 325°F.

Combine the orange zest and juice, the lime zest and juice, and the honey, salt, and pepper in a small bowl. Cover and refrigerate until ready to use.

Remove the turkey breast from the package, and pat it dry with paper towels. Discard the gravy packet or wash it and refrigerate it for another use. Lift the string netting and shift its position on the turkey breast for easier removal after cooking. Place the turkey breast on a flat roasting rack in a 3-inch-deep roasting pan. Rub the turkey with olive oil.

Bake the turkey for 1¾ to 2 hours, brushing it several times with the citrus mixture during the last 30 minutes of baking. The turkey is done when the meat registers 170°F when an instant-read thermometer is inserted in the center of the roast. Let the turkey stand for 10 minutes before removing the string netting and carving.

BLACKBERRY PORK CHOPS

THESE DAYS IT IS RARE to find people who raise their own meat for the table, but it hasn't been that many generations since most Americans lived on farms and grew all their own food. Prior to refrigeration, meat such as pork was served fresh in the fall and winter. Farmers would wait until temperatures cooled, so the pork would keep through the winter. Around Thanksgiving or soon afterward, my grandparents would process their meat, but it had to wait until the corn had been put up in the crib, the apples were picked, all the canning was done, and the fall plowing was finished.

They had preferences on how they cut their meat, and they always had nice thick pork chops. I remember how good those were back then, and I still like them that way. When you cook a thick chop, it's important to go slow so you don't overcook it, or it will be dry. Letting the chops simmer in their own juices helps keep the meat moist. The crowning glory of this recipe is the sweet tang of the blackberry gastrique, a thick sauce made with a reduction of vinegar, sugar, and blackberries. It adds just the right accent to the flavor of the chops.

Spray a wide nonreactive skillet with nonstick cooking spray and set it over medium-high heat. Arrange the pork chops in the skillet and sprinkle them generously with pepper. Brown the meat well on both sides, 8 to 10 minutes total.

Reduce the heat to medium-low, cover the skillet, and cook until the chops are still moist and look slightly pink in the center, 6 to 8 minutes. Lift the chops onto a platter and keep warm.

Over medium heat, add the brown sugar and water to the fat and drippings left in the skillet. Stir, allowing the mixture to caramelize, 3 to 4 minutes. Then add the blackberries, vinegar, sea salt, and pepper, and cook, stirring, until the consistency becomes syrup-like, 5 to 7 minutes.

Transfer the pork chops to a serving platter, and pour the blackberry gastrique over them. Garnish with fresh blackberries, and serve.

SERVES 6

6 thick center-cut pork chops (about 2 pounds total), trimmed of fat

Freshly ground black pepper

FOR THE BLACKBERRY GASTRIQUE

1 tablespoon light brown sugar

2 tablespoons water

½ cup fresh or frozen blackberries

4½ teaspoons balsamic vinegar

½ teaspoon sea salt

¼ teaspoon cracked black pepper

½ cup fresh blackberries, for garnish

SPICED RED CABBAGE WITH APPLES AND THYME

THERE ARE SOME RECIPES with names that suggest the best time of year to serve them. This is one of those recipes. In the cool days of fall, the red cabbages in my garden are gorgeous red orbs and the apple crop is at its peak of flavor. What better time to put together this memorable combination? I enjoy the aroma of this dish as it bakes in the oven, becoming warm and bubbly. It's a flavorful blend of sweetness from the apples and brown sugar, tang from the orange zest, and a spicy hint of herbs from the thyme. This dish is perfect with pork chops or a nice pork roast.

Preheat the oven to 400°F.

Combine all the ingredients except the salt and pepper in a large, heavy Dutch oven, and mix well. Bake, covered, for 1 hour, or until the cabbage is tender.

Transfer the Dutch oven to the stovetop and cook, uncovered, over medium heat, stirring frequently, for 5 minutes or until the liquid thickens slightly. Season with the salt and pepper, and serve.

SERVES 8

2 pounds red cabbage, cored and shredded

1 pound tart sweet apples (such as Arkansas Black, Fuji, or Granny Smith), peeled, cored, and finely chopped

1 large sweet onion, finely chopped

3 garlic cloves, finely chopped

½ cup dry red wine

½ cup fresh orange juice

2 tablespoons red wine vinegar

2 tablespoons dark brown sugar, packed

1 tablespoon grated orange zest

2 tablespoons fresh thyme leaves, finely chopped

2 teaspoons salt

1 teaspoon freshly ground black pepper

GOLDEN COUSCOUS WITH PINE NUTS

SERVES 6

1 cup couscous

¾ cup chopped dried apricots

¾ cup golden raisins

2 shallots, finely chopped

1½ tablespoons ground cumin

1½ teaspoons ground coriander

1½ teaspoons salt, plus more if needed

½ teaspoon freshly ground black pepper, plus more if needed

Boiling water

Grated zest and juice of 2 oranges

⅔ cup pine nuts, toasted

½ cup chopped fresh flat-leaf parsley leaves

A FRIEND IN ENGLAND shared this recipe for couscous dressed with citrus, raisins, and pine nuts. Many of the meals I enjoyed while I was living there as a student boasted flavors from Africa, the Middle East, and beyond. Coming from more of a "meat and potatoes" family, it was a new taste, which I really enjoyed.

Couscous is actually a pasta, not a grain. It is made by mixing semolina (coarsely ground durum wheat) and water, and then shaping that into the little "grains" of pasta. The pasta is then coated with flour to prevent the grains from sticking to each other. This dish doesn't require a lot of time and can be stored in the fridge well before you plan to serve it—chilled, at room temperature, or slightly warmed. I think it's particularly lovely with pork or anything off the grill.

Put the couscous in a heatproof bowl, and add the apricots, raisins, shallots, spices, and salt and pepper. Add enough boiling water to the orange juice to equal 2½ cups of liquid, and pour this over the couscous. Stir in the orange zest. Cover, and set aside for 10 to 15 minutes.

Add the toasted pine nuts and the parsley, and fluff the couscous with a fork to combine the ingredients. Taste, and add more salt and pepper if necessary. Serve hot, at room temperature, chilled, or rewarmed in the microwave oven.

WHITE CHEDDAR PARSNIPS AND POTATOES

I'M ON A CAMPAIGN FOR PARSNIPS, and here's why: Parsnips are beautiful. They resemble a large ivory-skinned carrot and have a royal history. In ancient Rome, parsnips were considered a luxury food for the aristocracy. And before potatoes were discovered in the New World, the parsnip was the favored root crop, prized not only for its long storage life but also for its sweet, nutty taste and nutritional value. So let's bring parsnips back to the garden!

This recipe is a good way to begin. These two root vegetables should get together more often on the plate. It's a mash made in heaven. Once you've tasted parsnips in this dish, you'll want to expand your repertoire. Try adding them to other vegetables in chicken stock to make a hearty soup. I think you'll enjoy their distinct flavor.

Place the potatoes and parsnips in a large pot, add the chicken broth, and cook over medium-high heat until they are fork-tender, 12 to 15 minutes. Drain the vegetables in a colander, and return the pot to the burner.

Add the half-and-half and butter to the hot pot, and stir until the butter has melted. Return the hot drained potatoes and parsnips to the pot and mash them, leaving some small chunks for texture. Stir in the cheddar cheese. Season with salt and pepper to taste. Gently reheat over low heat, if necessary.

Transfer the parsnip-potato mash to a warm serving bowl, and sprinkle with the crumbled bacon and snipped chives. Serve hot.

SERVES 6

- 3 to 4 medium russet potatoes (about 2 pounds total), peeled and cut into 1-inch cubes
- 4 to 6 medium parsnips (about 1 pound total), peeled, cut into 2-inch lengths, large ends cut in half lengthwise
- 4 cups chicken broth
- ½ cup half-and-half or whole milk
- 4 tablespoons (½ stick) butter
- 6 ounces white cheddar cheese, shredded (1½ cups)
- Kosher salt and freshly ground black pepper
- 4 slices bacon, cooked crisp and crumbled
- 2 tablespoons snipped fresh chives

GOAT CHEESE AND LEEK TART

MY FIRST TASTE OF FRESH HOMEGROWN LEEKS was during my first year in college. We were studying the classification of plants and my biology professor, Dr. Clark, brought in an armload of these gorgeous vegetables to illustrate a member of the *Allium* genus. It was around mid-October, and I was surprised at how many leeks he still had in his garden. Later, I began growing my own supply of the delectable beauties. Once I discovered their mild, delicate flavor, I haven't been able to let a season pass without planting a few rows.

Tender sweet leeks and tangy goat cheese are delicious partners in this rich savory tart. It's easy to prepare, and delicious as a brunch dish. Add a cup of soup and a salad for a great supper, or cut the tart into thin slices for a delightful appetizer.

Place a baking sheet on the center shelf of the oven, and preheat the oven to 375°F.

Very lightly butter the bottom and sides of a 9-inch-diameter tart pan with a removable bottom. Roll out the dough and press it lightly but firmly over the bottom and up the sides of the tart pan, being careful not to stretch it. Trim the edges, and then press the dough up about ¼ inch above the rim of the pan all around. Prick the bottom all over with a fork. Brush some of the beaten egg over the dough.

Place the pan on the baking sheet and bake for 20 to 25 minutes, until the pastry is golden. Check halfway through the cooking time to make sure that the pastry isn't rising up in the center. If it is, just prick it a couple of times and gently press it back down with the back of a fork. When the crust is done, remove the tart pan but leave the oven on.

While the crust is baking, prepare the filling: Cut off the tough green tops of the leeks, leaving 2 to 3 inches of the tender green portion. Then make a vertical split down the center of each leek, and wash the leeks thoroughly to remove any sand or grit. Cut the leeks into ¼-inch-thick slices.

Melt the butter in a skillet over medium-low heat, and add the leeks,

recipe continues

SERVES 8

Dough for 1 Easy Pie Crust (page 130)

4 large eggs, beaten

2 pounds leeks (about 2 medium leeks)

4 tablespoons (½ stick) butter

1 14-ounce can artichoke hearts, drained and chopped

½ cup snipped fresh chives (½-inch pieces)

1 teaspoon salt

½ teaspoon freshly ground black pepper

¼ teaspoon freshly grated nutmeg

½ cup crumbled goat cheese

1 cup Greek yogurt

artichoke hearts, chives, salt, pepper, and nutmeg. Cook gently, uncovered, for 10 to 15 minutes or until tender. Remove the skillet from the heat.

In a medium bowl, whisk together the goat cheese, yogurt, and remaining beaten eggs. Add the leek mixture and blend well. Pour the mixture into the baked tart crust, and return it to the oven. Bake the tart for 30 to 35 minutes, or until it's firm in the center and the surface has turned a nice golden brown. Remove it from the oven and allow it to rest for 10 minutes before serving (this makes it easier to cut into portions).

The best way to remove the tart from the tart pan is to ease the edge from the side of the pan with a small knife, and then place the pan on an upturned jar or a large can, which will allow you to carefully ease the ring away from the tart. Next, slide a long, thin knife between the pan base and the tart, and ease the tart onto a flat plate or board (or you can cut the tart into serving portions straight from the pan's base). Serve warm.

One of my favorite leek varieties, 'Giant Musselburgh', originated in Scotland. It is a hardy plant with long, thick stems and dark leaves. I also grow 'Pandora' and 'Autumn Giant'. Because leeks keep so well in the winter, I plant them late in the summer growing season and enjoy using them in recipes until spring. It's rarely too late to harvest a leek; they are cold-hardy down to about 5°F. Just be sure to harvest them all before spring's warm temperatures cause them to start growing again.

POTATOES AND GREEN BEANS WITH BLUE CHEESE AND WALNUTS

GROWING POTATOES IS ACTUALLY EASIER than you think. A fun project for kids is to take potatoes that have gone a bit soft and are pushing out their "eyes" and plant them in bushel baskets. Just cut out the bottom of the basket, fill it half-way with soil, and pitch in about three pieces of potato, spacing them 8 inches apart. Cover them up with soil, keep the soil consistently moist, and in 95 to 110 days you'll have potatoes.

I've started potatoes in the garden as late as September and had an abundant crop to harvest in November. The plants love the cool temperatures and extra mois-ture; after all, they are native to the mountains of Peru. I also plant a late crop of green beans. That is how this combination came together.

Now, if you'd asked my mom or grandmother how many green beans they needed, they would have likely said, "Oh, just a mess." So, just exactly what is a mess? Best I can figure, a mess is about what you need for a meal, and a mess can vary according to the number of people you're feeding!

You can't go wrong with this recipe because you've got two sets of delicious companions conspiring together. Potatoes and green beans are a classic, and top-ping them with blue cheese and toasted walnuts makes them just that much better.

SERVES 6

12 red potatoes
(2 pounds total)
2 pounds green beans
½ cup walnut pieces
2 tomatoes, cut into
1-inch cubes
2 tablespoons spicy
brown mustard
¼ cup olive oil
¼ cup rice vinegar
1 teaspoon salt
½ teaspoon freshly
ground black pepper
½ cup crumbled blue
cheese

Place the red potatoes in a microwave-safe dish, and add ½ inch of water. Cover, and microwave on high power for 5 minutes. Check for doneness. If a knife does not pierce a potato easily, continue to microwave in 2-minute increments until done. Do not overcook; the potatoes should still hold their shape and be slightly firm. Remove them from the dish, drain, and set them aside to cool.

While the potatoes are cooling, trim the ends off the green beans and cut the beans into 1-inch pieces on the diagonal. Set them aside.

recipe continues

Preheat the oven to 300°F.

Place the walnuts on a small ovenproof pan and toast them in the oven for about 15 minutes, until they are just beginning to brown. Remove and set aside.

Place the green beans in the same dish that was used to cook the potatoes. Add ¼ inch of water, cover, and microwave on high power for about 3 minutes, until the beans are cooked but still crisp and bright green. Drain, and set aside.

Cut the cooled potatoes into 1-inch cubes. In a large bowl, whisk together the mustard, olive oil, rice vinegar, salt, and pepper. Add the potatoes, green beans, and tomatoes to the vinaigrette, and toss to coat. Transfer the mixture to a serving dish, sprinkle with the blue cheese and toasted walnuts, and serve at room temperature.

MORNING GLORY MUFFINS

IF YOU WANT TO IMPRESS YOUR HOUSEGUESTS, whip up a batch of these muffins. You can make them ahead of time and warm them in the microwave. The aroma is out of this world. In fact, I once used them as a kind of alarm clock. Guests were staying with me for the weekend, and they had a tendency to sleep away half the morning. I'm more of an early riser, so I discovered that all I needed to do was warm up the muffins and let their rich fragrance make its way to their room, and before you knew it, they would appear in the kitchen looking for that first cup of coffee and asking for a taste of "whatever smells so good." The only downside I've found with these muffins is that it's hard not to slather them with a little too much softened butter and homemade strawberry jam. But I guess that's something I'll have to learn to live with!

MAKES 18 MUFFINS

2 cups all-purpose flour

1 cup sugar

2 teaspoons baking soda

2 teaspoons ground cinnamon

½ teaspoon freshly grated nutmeg

½ teaspoon salt

2 cups finely shredded carrots

½ cup golden raisins

½ cup walnuts, toasted and chopped

½ cup shredded sweetened coconut

1 large Granny Smith apple, peeled, cored, and chopped

3 large eggs

⅔ cup vegetable oil

Preheat the oven to 350°F. Spray 18 muffin cups with a flour-based baking spray such as Baker's Joy, or line them with paper liners.

In a large bowl, mix together the flour, sugar, baking soda, cinnamon, nutmeg, and salt, blending well. Add the carrots, raisins, walnuts, coconut, and apple, and stir well.

In a separate bowl, combine the eggs and the oil. Add this to the flour mixture, mixing just until all the ingredients are moistened. Do not overmix. The batter will be stiff.

Fill the muffin cups two-thirds full, and bake for 20 to 25 minutes or until the tops are brown and a toothpick inserted in the center comes out clean. Remove from the oven and leave in the pan to cool for 10 minutes, then cool completely on a wire rack. Serve warm.

These muffins freeze well in a zip-top plastic bag for up to 3 months and can be reheated in the microwave once thawed.

CORN STICKS

MAKES 12 STICKS

1½ cups white cornmeal
¼ cup all-purpose flour
1 teaspoon salt
1 teaspoon baking soda
1¾ cups buttermilk
1 egg, beaten
2 tablespoons bacon
    drippings, melted

IN MY FAMILY, good cornbread is a point of pride. Typically it is cooked in a big cast-iron skillet that has been seasoned for years for the sole purpose of making cornbread. You can quickly ruffle a cook's feathers by using his or her cornbread skillet for another purpose. And if you want to see some real fireworks, put the skillet in the sink and start scrubbing away. Engaging in such an act is a sure way to reveal your lack of skill in the Southern kitchen.

I'll never forget the first time Mom served cornbread baked in a cast-iron corn stick pan. The bread came out looking like little ears of corn—how cool was that! So I made sure that when it was time to pass along this well-seasoned pan to the next generation, it ended up in my kitchen. When baked in this pan, the bread comes out extra-crunchy, which I love.

Here are a few tips about using a corn stick pan: You want to get the right amount of batter in the corn molds so it doesn't spill all over the pan, so I suggest filling them three-quarters full. You might try using a nylon turkey baster with the opening cut slightly larger to administer the batter. Neat freaks love this technique because it's so tidy.

Place two corn stick pans on the center rack and preheat the oven to 425°F.

In a medium bowl, mix together the cornmeal, flour, salt, and baking soda. Stir in the buttermilk and egg.

Remove the hot pans from the oven and brush each mold with about ½ teaspoon of the melted bacon drippings. Return the pans to the oven for approximately 2 minutes, or until the drippings are very hot.

Remove the pans once again and spoon the cornbread batter into the molds, filling them about three-quarters full. Bake for 18 to 22 minutes, or until golden brown.

Immediately remove the corn sticks from the pans, and place them in a bread basket to serve.

SWEET POTATO BREAD

MAKES TWO 9-INCH LOAVES

12 tablespoons (1½ sticks) butter, at room temperature

1½ cups sugar

1 cup dark brown sugar, packed

4 eggs, beaten

3 cups all-purpose flour

1 teaspoon salt

2 teaspoons baking soda

1 cup buttermilk

1 cup cooked mashed sweet potatoes (see sidebar, opposite)

1 tablespoon vanilla extract

½ teaspoon ground nutmeg

½ teaspoon ground cinnamon

½ teaspoon ground ginger

1 cup chopped pecans, toasted (if you used salted nuts, back off the salt to ½ teaspoon)

EVERY FALL WHEN I AM DIGGING UP my sweet potatoes from the garden, I can't help but think about how long humans have been enjoying the flavor of these vegetables. Evidence found in Peruvian caves reveals they have been part of our diet for more than 10,000 years! And they are a well-traveled spud. Christopher Columbus brought sweet potatoes to Europe after his first voyage to the New World in 1492, and other explorers transported them to the Philippines, Africa, India, Indonesia, and southern Asia. Since colonial times, sweet potatoes have been cultivated in the southern United States, where they remain a staple ingredient in the traditional cuisine. I'm delighted they made it around the world and back again!

Sweet potatoes blend easily with herbs, spices, and other flavorings to add their wholesome goodness to everything from main dishes to desserts. I've been making sweet potato bread for some time, and this is one of my favorite recipes. The bread turns out a pretty orange color, and the taste is rich and sweet, perfect with a slather of cream cheese.

Preheat the oven to 350°F. Butter and flour two 9-inch loaf pans, and set them aside.

In a large mixing bowl, cream together the butter and both sugars. Add the eggs, flour, and salt, and mix well. In a small bowl, stir the baking soda into the buttermilk; then add that mixture to the batter. Mix in the sweet potatoes, vanilla, and all the spices. Blend well, and then add the nuts, folding them in until they are evenly distributed in the batter.

Divide the batter between the two loaf pans, and bake for 45 to 55 minutes, until a toothpick inserted in the center comes out clean. Let the loaves cool in the pans for 10 minutes, and then remove them to a wire rack to cool completely. Slice, and serve.

If you don't have leftover mashed sweet potatoes on hand, you can either bake one for this recipe or use canned sweet potatoes.

To bake a sweet potato, wrap it in aluminum foil and bake it in a 350°F oven (using the same temperature you'll need for the bread) for 45 to 50 minutes, until good and tender. Alternatively you can wash the potato, pierce the skin with a fork in a few places, place it on a paper towel, and microwave it on high power for about 4 minutes. Then scoop out the cooked flesh for the bread recipe.

If you use canned sweet potatoes, just drain off the liquid and mash them.

PEAR SORBET

I HAVE A FRIEND who sends me a gift box of fresh fruit in the fall, and I have to say my favorite among them is those luscious, sweet, tender, delectable pears. This recipe is a great way to put them to use. The sorbet can be made in advance of a gathering and kept in the freezer. If it's not too late in the season, I'll collect some fresh mint or some rosemary to add as a little garnish. I also like to serve this icy treat with a nice crunchy cookie from my Aunt Jamie's box of recipes (see page 180).

SERVES 4 TO 6

2 pounds ripe Bartlett or Anjou pears, cored, peeled, and chopped

1½ cups extra-dry sparkling wine or pear juice

¾ cup sugar

1 tablespoon finely chopped crystallized ginger

2 tablespoons light corn syrup

Put the pears and ¾ cup of the sparkling wine in a medium saucepan and bring to a boil over medium-high heat. Then lower the heat to maintain a steady simmer and cook, stirring occasionally, until the pears are tender, about 10 minutes. Add the sugar and crystallized ginger to the pear mixture, transfer it all to a blender, and puree until smooth. Stir in the corn syrup. Then pour the mixture into a container, cover, and chill.

When the mixture is cold, stir in the remaining ¾ cup sparkling wine. Freeze it in an ice cream maker, following the manufacturer's instructions.

Serve immediately, or transfer to a freezer-safe container, cover, and freeze until ready to serve. (If serving the sorbet after it has been frozen in your freezer, remove it from the freezer 10 to 15 minutes before dishing it out, so it has some time to thaw a little.)

AUNT JAMIE'S COOKIES

MAKES 6 DOZEN

1 cup (2 sticks) butter,
  at room temperature

1 cup granulated sugar

1 cup firmly packed light
  brown sugar

1 large egg

1 cup vegetable oil

1 tablespoon vanilla
  extract

1 cup rolled oats

1 cup crushed corn
  flakes

½ cup shredded
  sweetened coconut

1 cup chopped pecans

3½ cups sifted
  all-purpose flour

1 teaspoon baking soda

1 teaspoon salt

THESE COOKIES ARE SO GOOD that I always make a big batch and freeze some. I keep them hidden in the back of the freezer, disguised as cut butter or extra baguette rounds. This way no one knows where the cookies are, so I can eat them all myself.

I've shared this recipe with friends who readily admit they are challenged in the kitchen. I tell them to try making these cookies because they are so easy and the yield is high. If they burn the first batch or two, they still have plenty of cookie dough for a quick recovery.

Preheat the oven to 325°F.

In a large mixing bowl, blend the butter with both sugars until creamy. Blend in the egg and mix together well, followed by the vegetable oil and vanilla extract. To this mixture add the oats, corn flakes, coconut, and pecans, stirring thoroughly. Mix the flour, baking soda, and salt; stir into the other cookie ingredients.

Put a sheet of wax paper on your work surface and place the cookie dough on top. Use a rolling pin to roll out the dough to a ¼-inch thickness. With a knife, cut the dough into triangles, about 2 inches long on each side. Place the triangles on an ungreased cookie sheet, and bake for 12 minutes. Allow the cookies to cool completely on the cookie sheet before removing them.

These cookies will keep at room temperature for a couple of weeks (if they last that long!) or for a couple of months in an airtight container in the freezer.

FROZEN COFFEE-GINGER MERINGUE CAKE WITH POMEGRANATE SAUCE

THIS IS WHAT I CALL COMPANY DESSERT—you know, one of those recipes you are always looking for that is guaranteed to get plenty of oohs and aahs when guests see it and even more compliments when they taste it. It is a heavenly, light dessert with a wonderful pomegranate sauce, divine with a really good cup of coffee.

Now, let's talk presentation. You want to time bringing out the cake. Wait until all the dishes have been cleared away and you have a nice stack of plates ready for the cake on the table. Make a big entrance, carrying the cake from the kitchen to the dining room. Cut one slice and then drizzle a little extra sauce on the serving, and ask the person next to you to pass it along. The wonderful aroma of the ginger in the cake will fill the air as it is passed to the person at the end of the table. It's a great way to build the anticipation of that first bite of such a delicious cake!

To save time, you can use store-bought meringues—it doesn't matter if they are powdery and dry. You'll need about 10 meringues that are approximately 3½ inches in diameter.

To make the meringues, preheat the oven to 225°F. Line a baking sheet with parchment paper and rub the paper with a trace of sunflower oil, or line the sheet with a silicone baking mat. Set the baking sheet aside.

Whisk the egg whites until they are very stiff and dry. Then slowly add the granulated sugar bit by bit, whisking until the egg whites regain their former stiffness. Fold in the superfine sugar with a large metal spoon. Spoon the mixture onto the lined baking sheet, and bake until crisp, about 3 hours. Remove, and break the meringues into pieces.

Mix the instant coffee with the boiling water, and then refrigerate until well chilled.

Whip the cream to the soft-peak stage, and mix in the sugar, coffee liqueur, and the chilled coffee. Fold in the broken meringues, the crystallized

recipe continues

SERVES 8 TO 10

FOR THE MERINGUES
Sunflower oil (optional)
6 egg whites
¾ cup granulated sugar
¾ cup superfine sugar

FOR THE CAKE
2 tablespoons strong instant coffee granules, such as espresso
1 tablespoon boiling water
3 cups heavy cream
4 tablespoons superfine sugar
2 tablespoons coffee liqueur, such as Tia Maria or Kahlúa
3 tablespoons finely chopped crystallized ginger
1 tablespoon light corn syrup
1 cup salted pecans, finely chopped

FOR THE POMEGRANATE SAUCE

¼ cup seedless raspberry preserves

1 cup pomegranate juice (store-bought or fresh)

Juice of 1 lime

1 heaping tablespoon arrowroot powder, mixed with 2 tablespoons cold water

Seeds of 2 pome- granates (see box)

ginger, and the corn syrup. Line the bottom and sides of a loaf pan with parchment paper. Evenly distribute the chopped pecans on the bottom. Spoon the whipped cream mixture on top of the pecans. Cover with foil and freeze for at least 24 hours.

To make the sauce, combine the raspberry preserves and the pomegranate juice in a small pan over low heat, and cook until the preserves have melted. Add the lime juice and bring to a boil. Then remove the pan from the heat and stir in the arrowroot mixture. Put the pan back on the heat and simmer gently, whisking, for a couple of minutes. Then let the sauce cool. When it has cooled completely, add the pomegranate seeds.

To remove the frozen cake from the pan, allow the cake to sit at room temperature for 10 to 15 minutes, then invert the cake onto a serving platter. Slice into ¾-inch slices, drizzle with the pomegranate sauce, and serve.

Not only do pomegranates impart a deliciously tart flavor, they also provide us with more antioxidants than blueberries, cranberries, and grapes. Natural antioxidants like those found in pomegranates help protect us against free radicals, which can come from air pollution, pesticides, and even alcohol. We grow 'Wonderful' and 'Sweet' pomegranate varieties at the farm.

To remove pomegranate seeds without making a mess, score the fruit with a sharp knife from top to bottom in four places, then split it open over a bowl of water. Gently pull out the seeds under the water; they'll fall to the bottom as the flesh floats to the top. Just skim the flesh off the top and strain the liquid through a sieve to extract the seeds.

ALLEN'S FAVORITE SWEET POTATO PIE

SERVES 8

Dough for 1 Easy Pie
  Crust (page 130)
1 cup mashed cooked
  sweet potatoes (see
  sidebar, page 177)
½ cup sugar
¼ teaspoon salt
½ cup rich milk (my
  mother always used
  evaporated milk; I use
  half-and-half)
½ teaspoon ground
  allspice
1 teaspoon vanilla
  extract
¼ teaspoon baking
  powder
2 eggs
1 tablespoon butter, at
  room temperature

UNBELIEVABLY, THERE ARE PEOPLE who don't like pumpkin pie. Being the fresh garden produce and dessert lover that I am, it's always a shock to me. So my next question to these people is to ask if they have tried sweet potato pie, a delicious alternative. It is prepared in a similar way to pumpkin pie, and sometimes I'll change up the recipe a bit and combine half pumpkin and half sweet potatoes. This makes for a splendid, mouthwatering sensation.

Now, if you serve sweet potatoes at holiday gatherings and find that they haven't all been consumed, I've found a great way to give them a second life: Mash them all up together, and follow this recipe. Use the mixture to fill individual mini tart crusts. Serve with whipped cream and some grated orange zest on top. No one will ever know that they are eating leftovers.

Preheat the oven to 375°F.

Fit the pie crust dough into a pie plate, as described on page 130, and crimp the edges. Set the pie shell aside.

Combine all the remaining ingredients in a large bowl, and whisk together thoroughly. Pour the filling mixture into the pie shell, and bake on a rack in the center of the oven until the pie is set, 40 to 45 minutes.

Let the pie cool on a wire rack, and then cut it into slices. Serve at room temperature.

KENT'S KILLER FRESH APPLE CAKE

I HAVE MANY FRIENDS TO THANK for the great recipes I've collected over the years, along with all the great memories we share of cooking together. After college, Kent, who was one of my classmates, and I cooked on a regular basis, preparing a lot of Julia Child recipes and trying to talk like her. One of my favorite Julia quotes was how she loved to have a "good chicken salad on toasted rye with a scotch and soda." This was often the scene for our get-togethers—lots of laugher and fun.

Kent came up with this great recipe for apple cake. I think the name says it all—it really is a "to die for" apple cake! You just won't believe how flavorful and moist it is. I guarantee that if you take this cake to a holiday gathering, folks won't leave you alone until you give them the recipe. It's that good.

Preheat the oven to 325°F. Grease and flour a tube pan or Bundt pan, or spray the pan with a flour-based baking spray such as Baker's Joy, and set it aside.

In a large mixing bowl, combine the granulated sugar and brown sugar with the vegetable oil. Then stir in the eggs and vanilla. Sift the flour into a separate bowl, and add the baking soda, salt, and cinnamon. Add this to the wet mixture. Fold in the nuts, raisins (if using), and apples. The batter will be thick.

Spoon the batter into the prepared tube pan, and bake for 75 to 90 minutes, or until a knife inserted in the center of the cake comes out clean.

Cool the cake in the pan for 10 minutes, then invert onto a cake plate. Top with drizzled butter or whipped cream, if you like, and serve.

SERVES 12 TO 16

1 cup granulated sugar

1 cup dark brown sugar, packed

1 cup vegetable oil

2 eggs, well beaten

2 teaspoons vanilla extract

2 cups all-purpose flour

1 teaspoon baking soda

1 teaspoon salt

2 teaspoons ground cinnamon

1 cup chopped walnuts or pecans

1 cup raisins or dried cranberries (optional)

4 cups chopped peeled tart apples (such as Granny Smith)

Melted butter or whipped cream, for serving (optional)

MISS BIG FIG TART

SERVES 8 TO 12

½ cup merlot wine

¼ cup balsamic vinegar

¼ cup light brown sugar

¾ cup fig preserves

Dough for 1 Easy Pie
    Crust (page 130)

1½ cups coarsely
    chopped roasted
    salted pecans

1 cup sheep's milk
    ricotta cheese

24 fresh figs, stems
    removed, figs split
    in half

ONE OF THE PLANT STARS at my Garden Home Retreat is Miss Big Fig. She maintains an important position as the focal point at the east end of the garden. When a visiting fruit tree expert saw the tree, she estimated that Miss Big Fig was nearly a hundred years old, which is quite believable given the girth of her trunk.

When I started designing the garden, Miss Big Fig was growing at another location on the farm and I was hesitant to move her, considering her size and age, but I decided to take the risk. It took a huge front-end loader and lots of manpower to get it done, but now that she's settled into her new place, she seems quite happy being doted on. I've even planted strawberries under her branches as an edible groundcover to cover the old girl's ankles.

Late in the summer season, she starts to produce an abundance of delicious sweet 'Brown Turkey' figs. These are gathered as soon as they are ripe and before the birds can spread the word that the figs are ready, as they seem to love them as much as I do.

While I use brown figs for this recipe, any type of fig will do. Depending on the variety, fig trees bear at different times throughout the season. Whether they are 'Celeste', 'Black Mission', or 'Chicago Hardy'—you name it, this recipe will work. The balsamic vinegar and brown sugar add to the autumnal essence of this tart, and the sweet ricotta cheese makes it even more delectable. Serve it with a nice big dollop of whipped cream or crème fraîche.

Preheat the oven to 350°F.

Combine the merlot, balsamic vinegar, and brown sugar in a small saucepan, and cook over medium-low heat until the mixture has reduced to about ½ cup, 15 to 20 minutes. Stir in the fig preserves, and set aside.

Spray a 9- or 10-inch tart pan with removable bottom with nonstick flour-based baking spray such as Baker's Joy. Press the dough evenly onto the bottom and up the sides of the pan. Spread the pecans evenly over the bottom of the crust; then scatter the ricotta, as evenly as possible, over the pecans. Next, arrange the figs to cover the pecans and cheese. Spread the merlot reduction evenly over the figs, and bake for 35 to 45 minutes, or until the crust is brown and the filling is bubbly. Remove from the oven and allow it to rest for 10 minutes.

The best way to remove the tart from the tart pan is to ease the edge from the side of the pan with a small knife, and then place the pan on an upturned jar or a large can, which will allow you to carefully ease the ring away from the tart. Next, slide a long, thin knife between the pan base and the tart, and ease the tart onto a flat plate or board (or you can cut the tart into serving portions straight from the pan's base). Serve warm.

WINTER

PARMESAN PARSNIP FINGERS WITH CHILE JAM DIPPING SAUCE

PARSNIPS ARE A WONDERFUL fall-to-winter root vegetable with a mild yet seductive flavor. I'm always amazed that so few people have tried them. In fact, when fried in batter they could be called a poor man's calamari. They are an overlooked and underused vegetable that deserves much more notice. Now, I'll have to admit, I was one of those who often passed parsnips by. But after preparing recipes like this delightful appetizer and the White Cheddar Parsnips and Potatoes on page 167, I have discovered how tasty they can be.

Growing parsnips, what I call my "slow-motion" crop, has taught me to have more patience. While most vegetables go from seed to harvest in about 60 days, parsnips take a full 120 to 180 days to develop their ivory-colored roots and another two to three weeks for them to emerge from the ground. I often forget where I've planted them, so now I mix radish seeds in the same row. The radishes sprout quickly, marking the line and breaking the soil crust. By the time the radishes are ready to pick, they leave just about the right amount of space in the row for the parsnips to develop.

SERVES 6

2 pounds parsnips

1 cup dry breadcrumbs

1 cup (4 ounces) Parmesan cheese, grated

1 egg, beaten

1 tablespoon water

½ cup all-purpose flour

1 teaspoon kosher salt

2 tablespoons olive oil

Chile Jam (recipe follows), for serving

Preheat the oven to 375°F.

Oil a baking pan and place it in the oven to get really hot.

Meanwhile, peel the parsnips and cut them into 3-inch-long wedges.

When the baking pan is hot, scatter the parsnips in it and roast them for 10 minutes. Remove the parsnips and let them cool slightly.

While the parsnips are cooling, mix the breadcrumbs with the cheese in a shallow dish. In a separate dish, mix the egg with the water. In a third dish, mix the flour with the salt.

recipe continues

Dip the parsnips, one at a time, into the seasoned flour, then the egg, and finally into the breadcrumbs, coating them completely.

Heat the olive oil in a skillet over medium-high heat. Add the parsnips and cook until brown and crispy on the outside and cooked through, 4 to 6 minutes.

Serve warm, with the Chile Jam for dipping.

CHILE JAM

MAKES ABOUT SIX 1-PINT JARS

1 pound very ripe
    tomatoes
4 garlic cloves

4 large dried red chiles
    (seeds left in if you
    want your jam hot)

1 2-inch piece fresh
    ginger, sliced thin
1½ cups superfine sugar
¾ cup red wine vinegar

Place half of the tomatoes in a food processor fitted with the metal blade, and add the garlic, chiles, and ginger. Process until pureed. Pour the mixture into a heavy-bottomed nonreactive saucepan. Add the sugar and vinegar, and bring the mixture to a boil, stirring slowly. Reduce the heat to a simmer. Cut the remaining tomatoes into a fine dice and add them to the pan. Simmer for 30 to 40 minutes, stirring from time to time. The mixture will turn slightly darker and sticky.

Ladle the Chile Jam into warm, dry sterilized jars, and seal with the lids while the mixture is still warm.

The longer you keep this jam, the hotter it gets. It keeps for about 3 months in the refrigerator.

NOTE: This jam is also good over cream cheese and served with crackers.

UNCLE MIKE'S EGGPLANT TAPENADE

IN MY FAMILY you don't have to be a blood relative to be considered kin. That's how it is with Uncle Mike. Although he isn't technically related, he is a friend who is a welcome addition at our get-togethers. He always brings lots of good food to share, often in jars that bear his own "Uncle Mike" label. One of his great-tasting creations is this eggplant tapenade. The Mediterranean blend of olives, onions, and peppers invites as many variations as there are cooks. Uncle Mike made it his own by adding eggplant and a special selection of spices. It's delicious spooned onto garlic and olive oil crostini or your favorite crackers.

At the end of the fall season, when the garden is loaded with peppers and eggplants, I like to whip up a batch of Uncle Mike's tapenade. In the spirit of his generosity, I prepare enough so I can give jars of it as Christmas presents, along with his recipe. I invite you to spread the joy and make some for yourself!

Combine the eggplant, onions, mushrooms, bell pepper, garlic, and oil in a large saucepan. Cover, and simmer over medium heat for 10 minutes.

Add all the remaining ingredients. Mix well and simmer, covered, for 25 minutes, stirring occasionally. The eggplant should be cooked but not overly soft.

Spoon the tapenade into clean jars or other containers with lids. Refrigerate for up to 2 weeks or freeze up to 2 months. Serve it at room temperature with a selection of your favorite crackers.

MAKES 5 CUPS

1 medium eggplant (unpeeled), finely chopped

1 large onion, coarsely chopped

½ cup coarsely chopped mushrooms

⅓ cup chopped green bell pepper

3 garlic cloves, minced

⅓ cup vegetable oil

½ cup chopped pimiento-stuffed green olives

¼ cup chopped ripe olives

¼ cup small capers, drained

1 6-ounce can tomato paste

¼ cup water

¼ cup red wine vinegar

2 teaspoons salt

1 teaspoon freshly ground black pepper

1 tablespoon finely chopped fresh oregano leaves, or 1 teaspoon dried oregano leaves

CRANBERRY SPICE COCKTAIL

MAKES 1 DRINK

SPICED SUGAR
½ cup superfine sugar
1½ teaspoons ground
   allspice

FOR THE DRINK
1 orange wedge (⅛ of
   the orange)
1½ ounces
   (3 tablespoons)
   Cranberry Spice
   Vodka (recipe
   follows)
½ ounce (1 tablespoon)
   Cointreau
1 teaspoon fresh lemon
   juice
1 tablespoon sparkling
   water
1 fresh or frozen
   cranberry, for garnish

I'M NOT MUCH FOR TRYING LOTS OF FANCY COCKTAILS—I tend to stick with wine and an occasional three-olive dirty martini. But during the holidays, I enjoy making this drink for my holiday parties. Serve it with savory nibbles such as Peppered Walnuts (page 137) or crackers topped with Uncle Mike's Eggplant Tapenade (page 193).

A bottle of the cranberry-infused vodka makes a wonderful gift for friends—with the cocktail recipe attached. Vodka has the ability to take on the flavors of other things. Saturating spirits with flavor is a great way to create your own unique blends. The basic concept is to marry a variety of choice flavors into a base liquor to create a custom-flavored spirit. In addition to vodka, other clear liquors, including gin, sake, and light rum, are also good choices.

Stir the sugar and allspice together in a shallow bowl, and set the mix aside. Chill a cocktail glass in the freezer.

Dip the rim of the chilled cocktail glass in the Spiced Sugar, and set the glass aside.

Squeeze the orange wedge into a cocktail shaker and then drop it in. Fill the shaker with ice. Then add the vodka, Cointreau, lemon juice, and sparkling water. Cap the shaker and shake vigorously. Strain the drink into the prepared cocktail glass, garnish with a cranberry, and serve.

CRANBERRY SPICE VODKA
MAKES APPROXIMATELY 750 ML

1 cup fresh or frozen cranberries	1 teaspoon whole coriander seeds, cracked	1 cinnamon stick, cracked
5 whole cloves		6 whole allspice berries, cracked
1 whole nutmeg, cracked	1 whole vanilla bean	1 bottle (750 ml) vodka

Place the cranberries and spices in a large jar with an airtight lid, and top with the vodka. Cover, and let the vodka infuse for 2 to 3 days at room temperature. Strain into an attractive container, and cover tightly.

HOT PEPPER JELLY

FOR THOSE WHO HAVEN'T HAD THE PLEASURE of tasting hot pepper jelly, the ingredients may sound a bit strange, but I'm telling you, it is positively addictive. It's made with both bell and hot peppers and lots of sugar. It's wonderfully sweet and hot at the same time.

I make it in the late fall, when the pepper plants are heavy with beautiful pods. Usually farmers at the market will have an abundance of peppers as well, so you can pick up whatever you need if you don't grow them yourself.

For a casual appetizer, spoon a generous amount of pepper jelly over a softened block of cream cheese and serve it with assorted crackers. Quick, easy, and delicious!

MAKES 6 PINTS

2 cups finely chopped green bell peppers

1 cup finely chopped jalapeño peppers

6 cups sugar

1½ cups apple cider vinegar

6-ounce container liquid pectin

Sterilize six 1-pint or twelve ½-pint canning jars and lids according to the manufacturer's instructions.

Combine the peppers, sugar, and vinegar in a large stockpot. Set it over high heat and, stirring constantly, bring the mixture to a full rolling boil; let it boil for 3 minutes, and continue to stir constantly. Then remove the pot from the heat and let cool for 5 minutes. Stir in the liquid pectin, and then let the mixture cool for 2 more minutes.

Quickly ladle the jelly into the warm, dry sterile jars, filling them to within ¼ inch of the tops. Wipe the lips of the jars clean. Cover the jars with the flat lids, and then screw the bands on tight. Set the jars aside to cool; then store at room temperature.

To keep the peppers more evenly distributed, I like to turn the jars over for a few seconds every 10 or 15 minutes while the jelly is cooling. You can substitute any color of bell pepper, or substitute any combination of hot peppers for the jalapeños, to make the jelly as mild or as hot as you would like it. As long as the jars are sealed, the jelly will keep indefinitely.

CARROT GINGER SOUP

IF YOU'RE LIKE ME, you love fresh carrots just about any way they're served, but I think a soup like this helps raise this root vegetable up to a higher level of appreciation. Too often, the carrot is the sidekick to lots of other things, but here it can stand alone and shine.

Carrots are a natural for eating in the fall and winter since most root vegetables can be stored easily, even in the ground. I really like the way fresh carrots look with their green tops. But if you're going to store them, remove the green foliage because moisture escapes through the foliage, taking water out of the carrot itself. This is particularly true of the small baby varieties.

The flavor of carrots and ginger together is a match made in heaven. This soup is delightful to the senses: the aroma is captivating, the color is appealing, and the flavors dance on your tongue. You can serve it either warm or cold. I like it warm, as a nice accompaniment to the Grilled Ham and Smoked Cheddar Sandwich on page 198.

SERVES 6

6 tablespoons (¾ stick) butter

8 large carrots, peeled and chopped

1 medium onion, chopped

2 celery ribs, including tops, chopped

3 garlic cloves, finely chopped

2 tablespoons grated fresh ginger

6 cups chicken broth

1 cup half-and-half, or to taste

1 teaspoon salt

¼ teaspoon ground white pepper

Sour cream (optional)

Cracked black pepper (optional)

Melt the butter in a large saucepan over medium heat. Add the carrots, onions, celery, garlic, and ginger, and sauté until the onions are soft, 10 to 12 minutes.

Add the chicken broth, bring to a boil, and then reduce the heat. Simmer until the carrots are tender, 8 to 10 minutes more.

Puree the mixture, in batches, in a blender or food processor until smooth. Return the puree to the saucepan and heat to boiling. Add the half-and-half, salt, and white pepper, and serve immediately. The soup is beautiful with a swirl of sour cream and a dash of cracked black pepper.

GRILLED HAM AND SMOKED CHEDDAR SANDWICH

SERVES 6

12 slices artisanal bread of your choice

Dijon mustard, to taste

1½ pounds thinly sliced peppered ham

24 slices canned pineapple, grilled

4 green onions, white and green parts, chopped

12 ounces smoked cheddar cheese, sliced or grated

1 jar Major Grey's Chutney (or other favorite)

Butter or light olive oil spray

ON THE LIST OF FAVORITE FOODS chosen by all the ten-year-olds in this country, I imagine grilled cheese sandwiches rank close to the top. I mean, what kid doesn't love this classic sandwich? My more adult version combines ham, smoked cheddar, grilled pineapple slices, a few green onions, honey mustard, and a dab of chutney. A sandwich like this can be dangerously good, and I almost always go for two! So to be on the safe side, have plenty of ingredients on hand if you are fixing this for a crowd. Try it with the Carrot Ginger Soup on page 197, or flip back to the fall section and make the Rosemary Cannellini Soup (page 147)— either one is a great combination for a cold winter day.

For each sandwich, spread one slice of bread with Dijon mustard and then stack it with peppered ham, grilled pineapple, green onions, and smoked cheddar cheese. Spread the top slice of bread with a generous portion of chutney, and place it on the sandwich.

Preheat a cast-iron skillet or griddle over medium-high heat.

Butter the outsides of the sandwiches (or spray them with light olive oil), and grill them in the hot skillet until golden brown on both sides, about 6 to 8 minutes total. Cut the sandwiches in half and serve while still warm.

WHITE CHILI

SERVES 6 TO 8

¼ cup olive oil

1 pound boneless,
 skinless chicken, cut
 up into small chunks
 (see Note)

1 onion, chopped

1 fresh poblano chile,
 seeded and finely
 chopped

6 garlic cloves, finely
 chopped

4 cups chicken broth

2 teaspoons whole
 cumin seeds (ground
 will not withstand
 long cooking as well)

1 tablespoon finely
 chopped fresh
 oregano leaves, or
 1 teaspoon dried

4 15-ounce cans great
 northern or cannellini
 beans, drained

4 ounces Monterey Jack
 cheese, shredded
 (optional)

2 tomatoes, chopped
 (optional)

2 avocados, sliced and
 tossed with lime juice
 (optional)

1 package tortilla chips,
 broken (optional)

WHEN YOU ARE RAISED ON TRADITIONAL CHILI, the idea of white chili almost seems like a violation of a family code. But for those who don't eat a lot of red meat, or who are just looking for something different, this is a terrific way to enjoy chili. The chicken, beans, and other seasonings will provide as much flavor and punch as any conventional chili. I often serve it on New Year's Day when people are trying to hold on to their resolutions to eat right and make healthier choices. I can start preparing it early in the day and let it simmer in the slow cooker until we're ready to eat.

Combine the olive oil, chicken, onions, poblano chile, and garlic in a large pot and sauté over medium-high heat until the chicken is cooked through, about 12 to 15 minutes. Use two forks to shred the chicken in the pot.

Add the chicken broth, cumin, oregano, and beans, and simmer until the chicken is tender and the flavors have blended, 30 minutes.

Ladle the chili into individual bowls, and top each serving with shredded Monterey Jack, chopped tomatoes, sliced avocados, and/or broken tortilla chips, if desired.

NOTE: I favor boneless breasts for their ease and lower fat content. In a pinch, I have simply removed the meat from a whole roasted chicken that I picked up at the market.

LENTIL AND LEEK SOUP

IN LATE WINTER, I often make this on "Soup Sundays" at the Garden Home Retreat. I start it in the morning by harvesting leeks from the garden, and I add some of my home-canned tomatoes. That's when the magic begins. When the soup begins to thicken, the aroma guides anyone entering the front door directly into the kitchen.

This is an easy recipe to expand to accommodate visitors who happen to drop by. Sundays are often blissfully slow around the farm, and this is a great soup to enjoy by the fire with cornbread and a salad. Try it with the Baby Beets on Arugula with Citrus Vinaigrette (page 208).

SERVES 6

3 tablespoons olive oil
½ onion, diced
1 large or 2 small celery ribs, finely chopped
1 carrot, finely chopped
1 large leek, white and tender green parts, cut in half lengthwise, well rinsed, and thinly sliced
2 garlic cloves, minced
1 quart home-canned tomatoes, diced, or one 28-ounce can diced tomatoes
1 cup red lentils, rinsed and drained
4 cups vegetable stock
1 bay leaf
2 teaspoons kosher salt
1 teaspoon freshly ground black pepper
Chopped fresh flat-leaf parsley leaves, for garnish

Heat the oil in a large saucepan over medium-high heat. Add the onions, celery, carrots, leeks, and garlic, and sauté until soft, 12 to 15 minutes.

Add the tomatoes, lentils, vegetable broth, and bay leaf, and bring to a boil. Then lower the heat and simmer, partially covered, for about 1 hour, or until the lentils are tender. Add the salt and pepper, and remove the bay leaf.

For a more rustic or informal meal, serve the soup as is. For a more "refined" meal, puree the soup in a food processor or blender until smooth, and then gently reheat it.

Ladle the soup into bowls, garnish with chopped parsley, and serve.

ROASTED SWEET POTATO AND FETA SALAD

I FIND IT INTERESTING TO SEE how our tastes change as we mature. When I was a child, one of the few things I wouldn't eat was sweet potatoes. Now, that violated two rules of the house: you had to at least try everything that was served, and you had to clean your plate. Abiding by those rules must have helped me overcome my aversion, because trust me, I have no problem eating sweet potatoes now. In fact, by grade school I had developed a voracious appetite for them. I recall my dad warning me, after going for my third helping, that I should watch it because Daniel Boone had eaten so many sweet potatoes that he had foundered on them and subsequently died. Even though I loved stories about Daniel Boone and watched every episode of the TV show starring Fess Parker, that didn't slow me down one bit.

While I didn't try this salad as a kid, as an adult I can truly appreciate the savory blend of the roasted sweet potato and the tart flavor of the feta. And since spinach is a cool-weather crop, if the winter is mild, I often have some fresh leaves that I can harvest from the garden.

SERVES 8

4 pounds sweet potatoes, peeled and cut into ½-inch dice

2 red onions, each cut into 8 wedges

2 teaspoons kosher salt

1 teaspoon cracked black pepper

¼ cup olive oil

FOR THE DRESSING

¼ cup red wine vinegar

2 tablespoons Dijon mustard

2 teaspoons honey

¾ cup olive oil

1 teaspoon kosher salt

½ teaspoon cracked black pepper

1 pound baby spinach, rinsed thoroughly and patted dry

6 ounces feta cheese, diced

Freshly ground black pepper

Preheat the oven to 350°F.

Combine the sweet potatoes, red onions, salt, and pepper in a large bowl and drizzle with the olive oil; toss to coat well. Spread the mixture in a single layer on a baking sheet, and roast in the oven for 30 minutes. Turn the vegetables, and continue roasting for 30 more minutes. The onions should be well cooked and caramelized and the sweet potatoes brown around the edges.

While the vegetables are cooking, combine all the dressing ingredients in a blender or food processor and process until combined.

Arrange the spinach in a shallow bowl or on a platter, and scatter the warm onions and sweet potatoes over it. (If the spinach wilts a bit, all the better.) Drizzle with the dressing. Scatter the feta over the top. Grind some pepper over the salad, and serve immediately.

APPLE AND CARROT SALAD

SERVES 6

¼ cup plain yogurt

¼ cup mayonnaise

1 tablespoon fresh
lemon juice

1 teaspoon honey

1 teaspoon kosher salt

1 teaspoon cracked
black pepper

3 large carrots

2 medium Fuji, Gala, or
Granny Smith apples

1 teaspoon poppy seeds

THIS IS A GREAT MAKE-AHEAD SALAD, as it is surprisingly good the next day. It is also a kid-friendly dish, blending the tartness of apples with the sweetness of carrots. Make sure you choose an apple with crisp flesh to give the salad a nice crunchy texture, and use the freshest carrots you can find. Carrots, being root vegetables, are tastier when they are grown in loose rich soil and have been recently harvested. You may be able to find carrots in different colors—deep red, bright orange, bold yellow—which would add some rainbow hues to the salad. The proportions of carrots and apples are flexible, depending on what you have on hand. If you like, toss in a handful of raisins.

Combine the yogurt, mayonnaise, lemon juice, honey, salt, and pepper in a large mixing bowl. Stir together until the mixture is well combined, and then set it aside.

Peel the carrots and cut them into matchsticks. Put them in a bowl. Next, quarter and core the apples, and cut them into matchsticks. Combine the apples with the carrots. Immediately add the carrots and apples to the yogurt mixture (moving quickly so the apples don't discolor).

Cover and refrigerate the salad for 2 hours or overnight. Just before serving, toss the poppy seeds into the salad.

I grow lots of apples at the Garden Home Retreat. Apples ripen at different times, so there are early, mid-, and late-season varieties. Some are best when eaten fresh, while others are better suited for cooking. The Rome Beauty, for example, is used primarily for baking because it has a firm, acidic flesh and tough, smooth skin. Late-season apples are often used for cooking, and most will last through the winter if stored just above 32°F. Some of my favorite winter varieties are Arkansas Black, Ashmead's Kernel, Braeburn, Cox's Orange Pippin, Fuji, and Calville Blanc d'Hiver.

CITRUS SALAD WITH POMEGRANATE DRESSING

SERVES 6

FOR THE DRESSING

⅓ cup extra-virgin olive oil

1 medium shallot, finely chopped

1 cup bottled pomegranate juice

2 tablespoons white wine vinegar

Salt and freshly ground black pepper, to taste

FOR THE SHALLOT RINGS

Vegetable oil, for frying

2 medium shallots, sliced and divided into individual rings

½ cup all-purpose flour

Kosher salt (optional)

FOR THE SALAD

2 romaine hearts, or other lettuce of your choice, chopped

8 orange segments

1 small red onion, sliced into thin rings

½ cup (2 ounces) Gorgonzola cheese, crumbled

1 pomegranate, seeds removed and set aside (see box, page 182)

Salt and freshly ground black pepper, to taste

MY PARENTS WOULD OFTEN RECALL that when they were growing up, the gift of an orange in their Christmas stocking was a special treat. Before shipping food long distances became common, fresh fruit was rare during the winter, so citrus was truly something special. Although there is an abundance of beautiful citrus in the market these days, fruit during the holidays still harkens back to a time when it was a luxury. This recipe will produce a refreshing salad that is also a treat for the eyes. The clean, tart taste is the perfect complement for roasted chicken and roasted winter vegetables. The pomegranate dressing adds both color and panache. Shallots are added two ways to this salad: first as flavoring in the dressing and then as fried rings that give the salad a nice crunch. The pomegranate seeds also lend extra flavor and texture.

To make the dressing, combine 1 teaspoon of the olive oil with the chopped shallots in a small saucepan and cook over medium heat, stirring occasionally, for about 3 minutes, until limp. Add the pomegranate juice and raise the heat to medium-high. Boil until the liquid is reduced to ¼ cup, 10 to 12 minutes. To prevent burning, be sure to keep stirring as the liquid becomes syrupy. Remove the pan from the heat and set it aside to cool. (Reserve the remaining olive oil, the vinegar, and the salt and pepper.)

While the pomegranate sauce is cooling, make the shallot rings: Pour about 1 inch of vegetable oil into a medium saucepan and place it over medium heat. In a shallow bowl, toss the shallot rings with the flour; then shake them in a mesh strainer to get rid of any excess flour. When the oil is hot (it will ripple), add the rings, stirring so they don't stick together. Fry the rings until they are crisp and brown, 2 to 4 minutes. Remove them with a slotted spoon, and let them drain on paper towels. Season the rings with a little kosher salt if you'd like.

When the pomegranate sauce is cool, pour it into a medium bowl. Whisk it with the vinegar and a few dashes of salt and pepper. Then slowly whisk in the remaining olive oil.

Toss the chopped lettuce into a serving bowl. Drizzle some of the dressing over the greens and toss lightly. (You may not need all of the dressing, but it will store in the refrigerator for about a week, so be sure to save it.) Add the orange segments, red onion rings, Gorgonzola, and salt and pepper, and toss to mix. Top with the shallot rings, and serve.

BABY BEETS ON ARUGULA WITH CITRUS VINAIGRETTE

SERVES 4 TO 6

12 baby beets (about 1 inch in diameter), washed and trimmed

CITRUS VINAIGRETTE

1½ cups fresh orange juice

2 tablespoons balsamic vinegar

1 teaspoon minced fresh thyme leaves

1 shallot, minced

⅔ cup extra-virgin olive oil

Salt and freshly ground black pepper

1 tablespoon extra-virgin olive oil

Salt and freshly ground black pepper

2 cups arugula leaves, rinsed thoroughly and patted dry

4 ounces fresh creamy goat cheese

¼ cup hazelnuts, toasted and coarsely chopped

ARUGULA IS ABOUT THE EASIEST THING I GROW. Just throw the seeds out on well-prepared ground, press them down so there's good seed-to-soil contact, water them in, and then stand back. Before you know it, the seeds have sprouted and the arugula is ready to harvest. I start picking the leaves when they are 2 to 3 inches long; that's when they have the best flavor.

Often referred to as the king of gourmet salad greens, arugula has dark green lobed leaves that have a sharp, peppery flavor. Since it favors cool temperatures, I plant plenty of arugula in the fall and enjoy it fresh well into the winter, particularly if I cover the bed with a frost blanket. It continues to thrive as long as the temperatures don't stay below freezing for a long stretch of time.

Adding some baby beets and citrus to these spicy greens makes for a punchy and delectable salad. And while you may think all beets are red, you can grow them or find them in farmers' markets in hues of gold, pink, and white, which adds some fun to the salad.

Preheat the oven to 350°F.

Place the beets in a small roasting pan and pour in enough cold water to reach about one quarter of the way up the sides of the beets. Cover the pan with foil and place it in the oven. Roast the beets until they are tender, about 2 hours.

While the beets are cooking, prepare the citrus vinaigrette: In a medium-size saucepan, bring the orange juice to a boil over medium heat. Then reduce the heat and simmer briskly until the juice has reduced to about ⅓ cup, 15 to 20 minutes. Pour the juice into a medium-size heatproof nonreactive bowl and let it cool to room temperature.

Once the juice has cooled, whisk in the vinegar, thyme, and shallots. Continue whisking while slowly adding the olive oil. Season with salt and pepper to taste. Cover the bowl with plastic wrap and refrigerate until serving time.

Check the beets for doneness: Carefully remove the foil from one side of the pan, opening it away from your face to avoid the escaping steam, and gently insert a skewer into a beet. The beets are done when the skewer slides in easily. Using a large spoon, transfer the beets to a heatproof dish and set them aside at room temperature until they are cool enough to handle.

Using a small, sharp knife, carefully peel the beets; their skins should slip off easily. Put the peeled beets into a mixing bowl, drizzle them with the 1 tablespoon olive oil, and season with salt and pepper to taste. Arrange the beets attractively around the edges of individual serving plates.

Put the arugula in another mixing bowl, drizzle with about half of the citrus vinaigrette, and toss well. Mound the leaves in the center of each plate.

Crumble the goat cheese over the arugula and beets, and sprinkle with the hazelnuts. Drizzle some of the remaining vinaigrette over the beets, and serve immediately.

IRON SKILLET FILET MIGNON

THE ESSENTIAL ELEMENT IN THIS DISH is not an ingredient but a good old-fashioned cast-iron skillet. If you don't have one, this recipe is as good a reason as any to get one. With a little TLC, a cast-iron skillet can last a lifetime, which makes it a great investment. As a cooking utensil, it is very versatile; you can use it on the burners to sear meat and in the oven to bake dishes. Best of all, with the proper seasoning, food doesn't stick to it, so it makes for a quick cleanup.

The cut of meat for this recipe, filet mignon (or the whole tenderloin), is my number one choice when it comes to beef. This is an easy way to prepare the filets when you have guests. The Roasted Sweet Potato and Feta Salad (page 203) and the Brussels Sprouts with Maple Mustard Vinaigrette (page 224) make delicious sides for these steaks.

SERVES 4

6 tablespoons Worcestershire sauce

6 garlic cloves, finely chopped

4 10-ounce filet mignons

Sea salt and cracked black pepper

Stir the Worcestershire sauce and chopped garlic together in a small bowl, and brush this over the filet mignons. Sprinkle both sides generously with sea salt and cracked pepper. Place the steaks on a plate, cover with plastic wrap, and marinate in the refrigerator for 8 to 12 hours.

Preheat the oven to 425°F.

Heat a cast-iron skillet over high heat. When it is very hot, add the steaks and sear them on both sides until browned, 3 to 4 minutes per side. Then transfer the skillet to the oven and roast for 10 to 15 minutes, or until an instant-read thermometer registers 130 to 135°F for medium-rare or 140 to 145°F for medium.

Transfer the steaks to a platter, and serve immediately.

To season a new out-of-the-box cast-iron skillet, just coat the inside with cooking oil and bake it in a 350°F oven for an hour. Then wipe it out with paper towels, and it is ready to use. You'll reinforce the nonstick coating every time you heat oil in the skillet. With time, the skillet will take on a beautiful black patina, which is the mark of a well-loved pan.

RUBBED BEEF TENDERLOIN

SERVES 10 TO 12

¼ cup plus 2 table-
spoons olive oil

1 tablespoon dried
thyme leaves

1 tablespoon dried
rosemary

4 teaspoons finely
chopped garlic

1 tablespoon coarsely
ground black pepper

2 teaspoons kosher salt

1 6-pound beef
tenderloin, trimmed,
silverskin removed

FOR THE WINE SAUCE

1 cup dry red wine

2 tablespoons finely
chopped shallots

Salt and freshly ground
black pepper, to taste

1 teaspoon fresh thyme
leaves

1 tablespoon butter

I GIVE CREDIT TO MY FRIEND TERI BUNCE for introducing me to the delicious combination of herb rub and wine sauce for beef tenderloin. This flavorful seasoning will yield outstanding results, but as with so many meats, it's all about the quality of the beef. So if you want to make a special meal, make sure you start off with a tenderloin that is worth the effort.

Beef tenderloin, also called beef fillet, can be an expensive cut. A whole trimmed fillet (about 6 pounds) may cost you a pretty penny—depending on its grade, quality, and where you buy it—but it will feed at least ten people with no bones or waste, so I find its value to be worthy of the price. This dish pairs perfectly with field peas and cheese grits, or better still, with the Brussels Sprouts with Maple Mustard Vinaigrette (page 224).

Preheat the oven to 425°F. Place a heavy-bottomed roasting pan in the oven and let it heat for 10 minutes.

While the pan is heating, combine the ¼ cup olive oil with the thyme, rosemary, garlic, pepper, and salt in a small bowl. Rub this seasoning paste evenly over the beef tenderloin.

Remove the roasting pan from the oven, and drizzle the remaining 2 tablespoons olive oil into the pan, tilting it to coat the bottom. Then add the seasoned fillet, place it in the oven, and roast for 10 minutes.

Turn the fillet over and return it to the oven to sear the second side for 10 minutes.

Reduce the oven temperature to 375°F and cook until the meat reaches the desired doneness, 15 to 18 minutes (an instant-read thermometer should register 130 to 135°F for medium-rare).

While the tenderloin is roasting, prepare the wine sauce: In a saucepan, combine the wine, shallots, and salt and pepper. Cook over medium heat until reduced by half, 15 to 20 minutes. Whisk in the thyme and butter just to heat through. Remove from the heat.

Remove the tenderloin from the oven and let it rest for 15 to 20 minutes. Then slice the tenderloin into ½-inch-thick slices and arrange them on a platter. Spoon some wine sauce over the top, and serve. Pass any extra sauce.

GRILLED PIZZA TOPPED THREE WAYS

SOME PEOPLE CONSIDER PIZZA to be its own food group because they love it so much. You don't have to leave home to enjoy the flavor of grilled pizzas with several kinds of toppings—this recipe makes it easy to prepare a variety of great-tasting pizzas at home, either on the grill or right in your own oven. Consider the toppings as starting points to inspire you to use your imagination. After all, that's one of the best things about making pizzas: you can put together all kinds of creative combinations to make it just as you like it.

The pizza dough takes a little time to rise, making this a perfect project for a winter weekend and a fun activity to do with friends and family. And if you are in a hurry, you can always purchase pizza dough from your local pizzeria or pick some up at the grocery store. But I encourage you to try making your own. Homemade and home-grown food is always best.

MAKES THREE 6-INCH PIZZAS

2 cups all-purpose flour, plus more as needed
1 envelope active dry yeast
1 cup lukewarm water
½ cup whole-wheat flour
1 teaspoon salt
Olive oil, for brushing
Toppings (see box, page 214)

In a large bowl, stir ¼ cup of the all-purpose flour, the yeast, and ¾ cup of the lukewarm water together. Set aside, uncovered, in a warm place until bubbly, about 30 minutes.

Stir the whole-wheat flour, the remaining 1¾ cups all-purpose flour, and the salt into the yeast mixture to form a soft dough. Then add the remaining ¼ cup lukewarm water, and blend together.

Scrape the pizza dough onto a lightly floured work surface and knead the dough, adding just enough all-purpose flour to keep the dough from sticking, until it is silky and elastic, about 5 to 7 minutes. Transfer the dough to an oiled bowl, turn it over to coat it with oil, cover the bowl with a clean kitchen towel, and let the dough rise until it has doubled in bulk, about 1½ hours.

Punch the dough down, cover it again, and let it rise for another 30 minutes.

Turn the dough out onto the floured work surface, and divide it into three pieces. Let the dough rest for 10 minutes.

recipe continues

Meanwhile, preheat your grill to medium-hot. Using your hands or a rolling pin dusted with flour, pat or roll each piece of dough to form an 8-inch round or oval that is about ⅛ inch thick. Brush olive oil over the surface of the dough and place it, oil side down, on the grill. Cook for about 1 minute, or the until dough is semi-cooked and has grill marks. Flip it over and cook the other side for approximately 1 minute. Remove the pizza crust from the grill and load it with your choice of toppings.

Place the pizzas on the grill, topping side up, tented with foil to melt the cheese. Once the cheese has melted, remove them from the grill. Let the pizzas rest for 3 minutes before slicing and serving.

Here are some topping suggestions:

- Meat and Cheese: caramelized onions, crumbled blue cheese, and strips of cooked steak
- Classic: red sauce, sliced cooked Italian sausage, pepperoni, and fresh mozzarella
- From the Garden: goat cheese and fresh or grilled fennel, bell peppers, mushrooms, and zucchini

SLOW-COOKER LAMB STEW

I KEEP A LARGE FLOCK of white Dorper sheep that I affectionately refer to as my organic lawn mowers. They keep the farm's paddocks and pastures clipped as close as a golf course, shearing off the grass with precision. The lambs are grass-fed and produce a variety of delicious cuts of meat.

There is nothing quite like this stew on a quiet winter night. It is delicious served with Corn Sticks (page 174) and a simple spinach salad. The key is to let the stew simmer just long enough so the ingredients blend into a lovely medley of flavors. If they are overcooked, the meat and vegetables become indistinguishable. This fine line makes for a great excuse to keep taste-testing the stew! Once that perfect flavor has been achieved, turn off the heat and let the stew rest at room temperature for the remainder of the day; then gently reheat it for the evening meal.

Pat the lamb dry with paper towels, and season it with salt and pepper to taste. Heat 1 tablespoon of the oil in a large skillet over medium-high heat until it is just smoking. Add half of the lamb and cook until browned on all sides, about 8 minutes. Transfer the lamb to a slow cooker, and repeat with an additional 1 tablespoon oil and the remaining lamb.

Add the remaining 1 tablespoon oil, the onions, and ¼ teaspoon salt to the skillet, and cook until the onions are lightly browned, about 5 minutes. Add the broth, 1¼ cups of the beer, and the brown sugar, thyme, chocolate, and bay leaves. Bring to a boil, using a wooden spoon to scrape up any browned bits. Transfer the mixture to the slow cooker.

Add the carrots, parsnips, and potatoes to the slow cooker, cover, and cook on the low setting until the meat is tender, 6 to 8 hours (or cook on high for 4 to 5 hours).

In a small bowl, whisk the flour and the remaining ¼ cup beer until smooth; then stir the mixture into the stew. Cook, covered, until the sauce thickens, about 15 minutes.

Remove and discard the bay leaves, stir in the parsley, and season with salt and pepper to taste. Serve piping hot.

SERVES 6 TO 8

4 pounds boneless lamb, trimmed of excess fat and cut into 1½-inch chunks

Salt and freshly ground black pepper

3 tablespoons vegetable oil

2 onions, chopped (about 2 cups)

4 cups chicken broth

1 12-ounce bottle Guinness Draught beer

1 tablespoon light brown sugar, packed

1 teaspoon dried thyme leaves, or 1 tablespoon fresh

1 ounce bittersweet chocolate, chopped

2 bay leaves

5 carrots, peeled and cut into 1-inch chunks

1 pound parsnips, peeled and cut into 1-inch chunks

1½ pounds (about 24) baby red potatoes, scrubbed and halved

¼ cup all-purpose flour

2 tablespoons minced fresh flat-leaf parsley leaves

ROASTED QUAIL WITH BERRY SAUCE

SERVES 4

FOR THE MARINADE
½ cup red wine
½ cup olive oil
½ cup finely chopped carrots
½ cup finely chopped celery

FOR THE QUAIL
4 quail, with the backs split so they lie flat
¼ cup olive oil
All-purpose flour, for dusting

FOR THE SAUCE
¾ cup dry red wine
⅓ cup chicken broth
2 tablespoons fresh lingonberries or cranberries
2 tablespoons butter
2 tablespoons finely chopped fresh flat-leaf parsley leaves
2 tablespoons dried thyme leaves

MY GRANDDAD WAS A CRACK SHOT, well known in the county for being an excellent marksman who always got his birds. Anyone who ever hunted with him quickly learned that he was also a vigorous walker. If you went hunting with Quenton Palmer, you'd better be ready to keep up. Even when he was well advanced in years, he could walk your legs off!

Pal, as we all called him, always kept a pen of beautiful bird dogs, all of them English pointers. He took great pride in them and would often say that he wished his kids would behave as well as his dogs. At the onset of quail season in late November, he and his dogs would head out into the crop fields and hedgerows in pursuit of these elusive birds. Hours and many miles later, they would return from their hunting jaunt with his jacket full of quarry. Then he'd spend the afternoon cleaning the birds, taking extra care to make sure all the shot was removed. Inevitably he'd miss a piece or two, so we learned to be careful whenever quail was served for supper.

This recipe for roasted quail comes from my friend Peter Brave, owner of Brave New Restaurant in Little Rock, Arkansas. The quail he serves is farm-raised, so no one has to worry about breaking a tooth on a piece of shot. I have followed his directions and serve it splayed, which just means that I cut the backs so the birds lie flat, and then I brown them in my cast-iron skillet and bake them in the oven. Since the birds are small, they cook very quickly. After the quail marinates, the cooking process only takes about 10 minutes or so.

The quail is so good prepared this way! The berry sauce gives it a taste of the season. If lingonberries aren't available in your area, cranberries are equally good. I often request a single quail as an appetizer when I visit Peter's restaurant. At home, I love to serve these quail on a large platter with roasted vegetables and pearl onions. It is the perfect centerpiece for an elegant yet rustic winter meal.

recipe continues

Mix all the marinade ingredients together in a bowl. Arrange the quail flat in a baking dish, and pour the marinade over them. Cover, and marinate in the refrigerator for 4 to 5 hours, turning the quail occasionally.

Preheat the oven to 400°F.

Pour the olive oil into an ovenproof skillet (preferably cast-iron) and heat it over medium-high heat until it is hot but not smoking.

While the oil is heating, remove the quail from the marinade, brush off the celery and carrots, and dredge the quail in flour, shaking off any excess.

Place the quail in the hot skillet and sear, moving them around so they don't over-brown, for 30 to 45 seconds on each side.

Transfer the skillet to the oven and roast the quail for 5 to 7 minutes, until the juices run clear. Transfer the quail to a serving platter and keep warm.

Discard the oil in the skillet, leaving just enough to barely coat the bottom. Immediately add the wine to the skillet (it will smoke, so make sure the vent is turned on). Add the chicken broth and the lingonberries. Bring to a simmer, stirring constantly. Add the butter, parsley, and thyme, and cook just until the mixture has thickened, 4 to 5 minutes.

Pour the sauce over the quail and serve immediately.

REVEREND SMITH'S HOLY DUCK GUMBO

EVERY YEAR FOR MY BIRTHDAY, my friend the Reverend Susan Sims Smith prepares a wonderful dinner. It is a celebration just the way I like it—low-key, with a small group of friends and plenty of good food. Susan's duck gumbo is the highlight of the meal.

As you can imagine, there are countless variations on the way this dish can be prepared. In fact, there is a World Championship Duck Gumbo Cookoff in Stuttgart, Arkansas, every year! I'm sure that if Susan entered the contest, her recipe would take the top prize; it is truly heaven-sent! Her gumbo is delightfully rich and draws the essence of its flavor from wild waterfowl. With all the flooded rice fields and two major rivers in the state, Arkansas is a duck hunter's paradise. Susan and I both know local sportsmen who are always generous in sharing their game.

Now, this isn't a recipe you can throw together in a few minutes. You will need to set aside some time to prepare it; but special recipes are always worth the effort. The great thing about gumbo is that it gets better over time. So my advice is to prepare it the day before the event. And don't be concerned if you don't have wild duck—the domesticated bird is equally delicious.

Place the ducks in a large stew pot, cover with lightly salted water, and bring to a boil. Simmer until tender, about 2 hours. Remove the ducks, and set the ducks and the stock aside separately.

Melt the butter in a heavy Dutch oven, and then whisk in the flour. Cook, whisking constantly over medium heat, until the mixture becomes a rich, warm brown, 5 to 8 minutes. Add the onions and celery, and stir with a wooden spoon until the vegetables brown, 4 to 6 minutes. Then add the garlic, tomato paste, tomatoes, bell peppers, green onions, ½ cup of the parsley, and the seasonings. Stir in 2 quarts of the reserved duck stock. (Add chicken broth or water to make 2 quarts, if necessary.) Boil rapidly for 30 minutes.

While the mixture is cooking, remove the meat from the duck carcasses and pull it apart into bite-size pieces.

Add the duck meat to the stew pot. (More duck stock may be added, depending on your preference.)

Pour the gumbo over hot cooked rice in soup plates. Sprinkle the remaining chopped parsley on top, and serve.

SERVES 10 TO 12

- 3 to 4 dressed wild ducks (about 2 pounds each)
- 8 tablespoons (1 stick) butter
- 1 cup sifted all-purpose flour
- 3 cups chopped onions
- 3 cups diced celery
- 3 garlic cloves, finely chopped
- 1 6-ounce can tomato paste
- 1 1-quart jar home-canned tomatoes, or 1 28-ounce can diced tomatoes, with their juices
- 3 cups diced green bell peppers
- 8 green onions, white and green parts, finely chopped
- 1 cup fresh flat-leaf parsley leaves, finely chopped
- 1 tablespoon finely chopped fresh oregano leaves, or 1 teaspoon dried
- 1 tablespoon finely chopped fresh thyme leaves, or 1 teaspoon dried
- 1 tablespoon salt
- 1 tablespoon freshly ground black pepper
- 1 teaspoon cayenne pepper

QUICK FRIED KALE

IT'S FUN TO TAKE A PLAIN JANE COOKING green like kale and turn it into a great-tasting side dish. The reaction I usually get when I serve this is "Wow, this is so good! What is it?" That's the response I'm looking for, because let's face it: kale needs a little dressing up. But once you grab a bunch and try this recipe, I'm sure you'll see these greens in a whole new way.

This dish might also entice you to try other cool-weather greens, including beet, mustard, and turnip greens, as well as Swiss chard, collards, and spinach. The flavors of these greens range from intensely earthy to spicy, and seem to invite the addition of assertive flavors, such as garlic, onions, smoky meats, sharp spices, and lemon juice or vinegar. These bold-tasting ingredients pair perfectly with the greens to mellow their earthiness and enhance their robustness.

SERVES 6

¼ cup olive oil

4 ounces pancetta, diced (about ¼ cup)

1 small onion, chopped

Pinch of red pepper flakes

1½ pounds kale, stemmed, leaves roughly torn, rinsed thoroughly, and patted dry

1½ cups low-salt chicken broth

1 garlic clove, minced

Freshly ground black pepper, to taste

Heat the oil in a large, heavy Dutch oven over medium-high heat. Add the pancetta, onions, and red pepper flakes, and sauté until the onions are deep golden, about 5 minutes. Add the kale, tossing the leaves with tongs to coat them with the oil. Add the chicken broth, and bring it to a boil. Cover, reduce the heat to medium-low, and simmer until the leaves are quite tender, about 10 minutes. (Thicker-leaved varieties will need longer, so check the pan, adding water or broth if needed, and taste a leaf.)

Stir in the minced garlic, raise the heat to high, and boil uncovered until the pan is almost dry. Season with a few grinds of pepper (you probably won't need salt), transfer to a platter, and serve.

When storing kale, avoid cramming the leaves into the back of the refrigerator. While they last longer unwashed, you're more likely to use them if they're recipe-ready. Remove bands from purchased greens, discard discolored leaves, and trim tough stem ends. Fill the sink with cool water, and swish the leaves in it. Repeat process if necessary. Shake off the moisture and let leaves dry on towels or in a salad spinner. Line the inside of plastic bags with paper towels, and lay the greens between the towels. Close the bag and refrigerate.

BRUSSELS SPROUTS WITH MAPLE MUSTARD VINAIGRETTE

SERVES 4 TO 6

2 pounds fresh Brussels
  sprouts

2 tablespoons white
  wine vinegar

2 tablespoons balsamic
  vinegar

2 tablespoons maple
  syrup

1 tablespoon coarse-
  grained mustard

½ teaspoon salt

¼ teaspoon freshly
  grated nutmeg

½ cup olive oil

Cracked black pepper,
  to taste

BRUSSELS SPROUTS ARE SAID to have been cultivated as far back as the thirteenth century in the vicinity of Brussels, Belgium, and have carried that name ever since. I've always been taken with how the vegetable looks like Thumbelina-size cabbages. The plant has a tall stem on which many tiny heads, or sprouts, form. Its cousins, green and red cabbages, make one large head at the top of a short stem, but if you cut the head of common cabbage from the plant, numerous tiny heads will grow from the remaining stem, in much the same manner as Brussels sprouts.

Some people find the assertive flavor of this vegetable unpleasant, but I've discovered that more often than not, the naysayers have had the unfortunate experience of eating Brussels sprouts when they were overcooked, which is the cause of that bitter taste. Prepared properly, they are wonderfully sweet and nutty, and they take well to being steamed, roasted, or sautéed.

If you are among those who are on the fence about the flavor of Brussels sprouts, this recipe might just give you that needed nudge.

Fill a large bowl with ice and cold water, and set it aside.

Trim the bottoms of the Brussels sprouts, discarding the outer leaves. Cut a ¼-inch-deep X in the stem end of each sprout (to ensure even cooking). Bring a large saucepan of salted water to a boil over high heat. Add the Brussels sprouts and simmer for 10 to 15 minutes, or until tender, stirring occasionally. Be careful not to overcook them! Plunge the sprouts into the ice water to stop the cooking, and then drain them in a colander.

Whisk the vinegars, maple syrup, mustard, salt, nutmeg, olive oil, and pepper in a medium bowl until thick and smooth. Add the Brussels sprouts and toss to coat. Transfer the sprouts to a serving bowl, and serve at room temperature.

The Brussels sprouts can be cooked and the vinaigrette prepared in advance. Just reheat the sprouts in boiling water or in the microwave, and then toss them with the vinaigrette.

SWEET ONION TARTLETS

SERVES 8

2 tablespoons olive oil

2 tablespoons butter

2 large sweet or yellow onions, sliced

8 green onions, white and green parts, sliced

3 garlic cloves, finely chopped

2 teaspoons fresh thyme leaves

Pinch of salt

Dough for Easy Pie Crust (page 130)

1 11-ounce package soft goat cheese

1 15-ounce can quartered artichoke hearts, drained

Salt and freshly ground black pepper

1½ cups heavy cream

4 eggs

½ teaspoon freshly grated nutmeg

ONE OF THE MOST MEMORABLE TARTLETS I've eaten was in a restaurant in Bar Harbor, Maine. It was so good, I marched right into the kitchen to ask for the recipe. I learned that the secret ingredients were capers, cloves, and a touch of nutmeg—an amazing amalgamation!

That inspired me to experiment with other tartlet recipes. I prepared six different variations for friends to sample so I could get their opinions as to which one was best. This is the recipe that won the blue ribbon. It's another great make-ahead dish: Once it's prepared, just stick it in the refrigerator. When you're ready, it takes just 30 minutes to cook. Add some soup and salad, and you have a great winter meal.

Preheat the oven to 350°F.

Heat the oil and butter in a large skillet over medium heat. Add the onions, green onions, and garlic, and sauté until they are caramelized and golden brown, 10 to 12 minutes. Stir in the thyme and the pinch of salt. Remove the skillet from the stove and allow the mixture to cool.

Meanwhile, divide the pastry into eight pieces. Roll each piece out on a highly floured surface to form a 5½-inch round about ⅛ inch thick. Gently press the rounds into eight 3½-inch tart pans. Roll the rolling pin across the top of each tart pan to trim the excess pastry. Prick the dough on the bottom of each tart pan with a fork. Place the tart pans on a baking sheet, and bake for about 10 minutes, until very lightly browned.

Remove the tart shells from the oven, leaving them on the baking sheet. Into each shell, place about 2 tablespoons of the goat cheese and 2 tablespoons of the artichoke hearts. Divide the caramelized onions evenly among the tarts, arranging them on top of the goat cheese and artichokes. Season with salt and pepper to taste.

In a mixing bowl, whisk the heavy cream, eggs, and nutmeg. Pour the mixture evenly into the tart shells, and bake for 25 to 30 minutes, or until the center does not jiggle. Remove from the oven, allow to set for 5 minutes, and serve warm.

SWEET POTATO GRATIN

SWEET POTATOES WERE AN IMPORTANT CROP for my grandparents and great-grandparents. Every year my grandfather, who we called "Pa Smith," would prepare the ground and plant several long rows of sweet potato slips—small rooted pieces of the vine that grow from the "eyes," or buds, of the potato. Once they took hold, the vines would carpet the ground, choking out any weeds in the way, and then they would erupt with lots of foliage and beautiful blossoms that looked like morning glories. Then, just before a frost was predicted, Pa Smith would cut back the vines because he believed that if there was a frost followed by a rain, water would follow the vines down into the ground and make black streaks on the potatoes. He must have known what he was doing because he grew some of the prettiest and best-tasting sweet potatoes around.

I'm continuing the family tradition at the Garden Home Retreat, where I plant 'Beauregard', 'Jewel', and 'Puerto Rico' sweet potatoes. There are over 400 varieties available, so you have plenty of choices. Generally, sweet potatoes are grown more in the South because they like it hot and need at least 100 days to mature. However, there are now varieties that mature faster, so I'd encourage you to give them a try even if your growing season is short. Most sweet potatoes are orange-fleshed, although white or very light yellow fleshed types were once considered the finest. Those are still available, although a little harder to find.

SERVES 6 TO 8

- 4 tablespoons (½ stick) butter
- 4 garlic cloves, minced
- 2 tablespoons all-purpose flour
- 1½ cups heavy cream
- 4 sweet potatoes (about 2¼ pounds total), peeled and cut into ¼-inch-thick rounds
- Salt and freshly ground black pepper
- ½ cup fine fresh breadcrumbs
- ½ cup freshly grated Parmesan cheese

Preheat the oven to 325°F. Generously butter a 1½-inch-deep gratin dish, and set it aside.

Melt 2 tablespoons of the butter in a small skillet over low heat. Add the garlic and cook, stirring, until it is softened, 3 to 4 minutes. Then add the flour and cook, stirring, for 3 minutes. Stir in the cream and bring the mixture to a simmer, stirring occasionally; remove from the heat.

Arrange the potatoes in layers in the gratin dish, seasoning them with salt and pepper to taste. Pour the cream mixture over the potatoes, and bake for 1 hour, or until they are tender. Remove the dish from the oven.

Melt the remaining 2 tablespoons butter, and mix it with the breadcrumbs and cheese. Sprinkle the mixture evenly over the potatoes, and return the dish to the oven. Bake for 15 to 20 minutes, or until the top is golden brown. Serve while hot.

SAVORY ROSEMARY BUTTERNUT SQUASH

WHEN IT COMES TO SQUASH, there are two general categories: summer and winter. So what's the difference? Basically it comes down to the skin. Summer squash—such as zucchini, scallop, yellow crookneck, and yellow straight-neck—is picked young, when the skin is tender and edible. Winter squash is picked fully mature, when it has a protective skin that is thick, hard, and inedible. Winter squash is higher in iron, riboflavin, complex carbohydrates, and vitamin A, but the edible skin of summer squash is loaded with beta-carotene.

Some of the more common winter squash varieties include butternut, acorn, delicata, buttercup, hubbard, and spaghetti squash. I'm partial to butternut; its sweet, creamy, dark-orange flesh and smooth, quick-peel skin make it versatile and easy to use. It is delicious blended with orange, lemon, balsamic vinegar, sharp cheeses, robust herbs, bold spices, or cured meats like bacon.

This dish pairs the squash with onions and apples, topped with a flavorful blend of apple liqueur, rosemary, and garlic, all roasted together until tender. It's a wonderful winter recipe because the kitchen fills with its warm aroma as it bakes.

SERVES 6

1 large butternut squash

1 onion

2 tart apples (such as Granny Smith, Gala, Braeburn, or McIntosh)

½ cup olive oil

¼ cup Calvados (apple liqueur)

1 teaspoon salt

½ teaspoon freshly ground black pepper

2 teaspoons finely minced fresh rosemary

2 teaspoons finely minced garlic

Preheat the oven to 350°F.

Cut the squash in half lengthwise, and then peel off the outer skin and remove the seeds. Now cut the squash horizontally, making ½-inch-thick slices. Cut the onion in half from top to bottom, remove the ends and skin, and then cut it into thin slices. Peel, halve, and core the apples, and cut each half to make thin slices.

In a 9 x 13-inch baking dish, arrange rows of slices in this order: squash, onion, squash, apple, squash, etc.

Mix the olive oil, Calvados, salt, pepper, rosemary, and garlic together in a small bowl. Drizzle the mixture over the squash, onions, and apples. Cover the baking dish with foil, and bake in the oven for 30 minutes. Remove the foil and bake for another 15 minutes, or until the squash is tender.

Remove the dish from the oven and transfer the medley to a serving dish. Serve immediately.

TINY ORANGE MUFFINS

MAKES 4 TO 5 DOZEN
MUFFINS

FOR THE MUFFINS

8 tablespoons (1 stick)
   butter, at room
   temperature

1 cup sugar

2 eggs, beaten

1 teaspoon baking soda

1 cup buttermilk

2 cups all-purpose flour

Grated zest of 2 oranges

⅓ cup golden raisins

⅓ cup chopped pecans

FOR THE GLAZE

Grated zest of 1 orange

Juice of 2 oranges

1 cup light brown sugar,
   packed

WHEN IT COMES TO SOMETHING that tastes as good as these orange muffins, I say live a little. If you are trying to watch your weight, this recipe is ideal because these muffins are miniature bursts of flavor. Given their size, you can enjoy one and it won't wreck your diet—but it may be a real test of your willpower. I can attest to that! The challenge is to stop at one.

The secret of the muffin's sweetness is the orange glaze. Once they come out of the oven, the tops are dipped in a mixture of brown sugar, orange juice, and orange zest. As the glaze dries, it gives the crust a slight crunch and some extra zip. If you're into the flavor of orange as much as I am, try adding a dab of butter and some citrus marmalade to make the mini muffins even more of a tasty bite.

Preheat the oven to 400°F. Generously butter mini muffin tins or line them with paper liners.

In a large bowl, cream the butter and sugar together. Then add the eggs and beat until well mixed. Dissolve the baking soda in the buttermilk, and add this to the mixture, alternating with the flour. Mix in the orange zest, raisins, and pecans.

Fill the muffin cups three-quarters full, and bake for 15 minutes. Immediately remove the muffins from the tins, and keep them warm on a serving plate.

In a small bowl, mix the orange zest, orange juice, and brown sugar. One at a time, pick up the warm muffins and dip the tops into the glaze. Let the muffins dry on a wire rack set over a baking sheet. Once they are dry, return the muffins to the serving plate and serve immediately.

GINGERBREAD WITH CITRUS FLUFF

SERVES 9

½ cup dark brown
sugar, packed

½ cup solid vegetable
shortening

2 eggs, beaten

1¼ teaspoons grated
fresh ginger

¼ cup unsulfured
molasses

1¼ cups sifted
all-purpose flour

¼ teaspoon salt

1 teaspoon baking soda

¼ teaspoon baking
powder

1 teaspoon ground
cinnamon

¼ teaspoon ground
cloves

½ cup hot water

Citrus Fluff (recipe
follows)

Twists of orange zest,
for garnish

LIKE MOST KIDS, my siblings and I were fascinated by gingerbread houses. We would beg my mother to make us one, not realizing how much time and effort went into putting a house together. Looking back, I can now see that she had her hands full just keeping up with the four of us running around in different directions. Then one Christmas, a big box was delivered to the house. Inside we found a beautiful gingerbread house from our aunt. It was huge and was covered with all sorts of edible decorations. The house made quite an impressive centerpiece, but when my mom finally gave us the green light to take it apart and eat it, we discovered it was hard and stale—probably it had been prepared in a warehouse back in the summer. Clearly, it was an object to be admired, not consumed!

Happily, this gingerbread recipe produces a cake that is quite the opposite. It is fresh, light, and oh so good with a strong cup of coffee or your favorite tea. It doesn't need sugarplums or fancy icing. That spicy goodness is all right there in the gingerbread, topped with a cloud of citrus fluff that will carry you away.

reheat the oven to 350°F. Butter and flour a 9-inch square baking dish, and set it aside.

In a large bowl, combine the brown sugar, shortening, eggs, ginger, and molasses, and blend together well. In a separate bowl, mix together the flour, salt, baking soda, baking powder, cinnamon, and cloves. Then gradually blend the dry ingredients into the molasses mixture. Add the hot water and stir until blended.

Pour the batter into the baking dish, and bake for 25 to 30 minutes, until a toothpick inserted in the center comes out clean. Allow to cool to room temperature. Slice into squares.

Spoon the Citrus Fluff onto the squares, and garnish each one with a twist of orange.

CITRUS FLUFF

MAKES ABOUT 2½ CUPS

1 egg	Grated zest of 1 lemon	1 cup heavy cream, whipped
½ cup sugar	2 tablespoons fresh lemon juice	
Grated zest of 1 orange		

eat the egg, sugar, citrus zests, and lemon juice together in a small saucepan. Cook, stirring, over low heat until thickened, about 5 minutes. Let the mixture cool completely. Fold the cooled mixture into the whipped cream, and chill.

NOTE: A time-saving tip is to substitute the egg, sugar, citrus zest, and lemon juice with 1 cup good-quality lemon curd (purchased at the store), and fold it into the whipped cream instead. Delightful!

JOSEPHINE FOSTER'S CORNBREAD DRESSING

SERVES 8

2 tablespoons bacon
  drippings

FOR THE CORNBREAD

1½ cups yellow
  cornmeal

½ cup all-purpose flour

2 teaspoons baking
  powder

1 teaspoon baking soda

1 teaspoon salt

1 egg, beaten

2 cups buttermilk

1 (6- to 7-pound)
  roasting chicken

8 tablespoons (1 stick)
  butter

3 to 4 celery ribs,
  including leaves,
  chopped

1 medium onion,
  chopped

5 green onions, white
  and green parts,
  chopped

12 slices day-old white
  bread, crumbled

1 cup half-and-half or
  evaporated milk

2 eggs, beaten

1½ teaspoons salt

1 level tablespoon
  rubbed sage

1½ teaspoons freshly
  ground black pepper

ONE OF THE BEST THINGS about the holidays is when everyone gathers and family stories are told. I enjoy how traditions are honored and passed along, and that includes family recipes. For many years I had no idea there was any other kind of dressing for a turkey than cornbread dressing. That's what was always served at all our holiday gatherings. In fact, it was just as important as the turkey.

Now, there are a lot of strong family opinions about the best recipe for this dish—and even more about whether it should be called dressing or stuffing. I can get a pretty good idea about where someone hails from by asking if they serve dressing or stuffing and what ingredients are used. I've found that more times than not, Southerners call it dressing and Northerners call it stuffing. Midwesterners commonly use white bread, sage, and raisins, while those who grew up in the coastal Northeast and mid-Atlantic areas often use oysters. And there are thousands of variations in between!

Our family has always prepared my great-grandmother's dressing, so it came to be known by her name, Josephine Foster. I had the good fortune of knowing her very well. She came by the recipe from her mother, Isora Tennessee Browne Crutchfield. My grandmother Kee Kee, who was Josephine's daughter, passed this recipe along to me in her own handwriting and I've kept it tucked away in one of her old cookbooks.

Now, if you've ever been in the kitchen with real good old-fashioned cooks, you know that they can rarely give you the exact amount of ingredients for anything. It's "a pinch of this" and "a dash of that" or a "oh, just a little of this will do." Even though Kee Kee watched her grandmother and her mother make this dressing, it was a real chore for her to try to sit down and think through all the ingredients, their quantities, and the steps. But I'm glad she did! If your family hasn't adopted a favorite holiday recipe for this classic dish, give this one a try.

Preheat the oven to 450°F. Place a well-seasoned 10-inch cast-iron skillet in the oven for 4 minutes, or until it is hot. Add the bacon drippings to the skillet.

Meanwhile, prepare the cornbread batter: Combine the cornmeal, flour, baking powder, baking soda, and salt in a large bowl. Add the egg and buttermilk, stirring well to combine.

Remove the hot skillet from the oven, and spoon the batter into the sizzling bacon drippings. Return the skillet to the oven and bake for 20 to 25 minutes, or until the cornbread is lightly browned. Remove the skillet from the oven and turn the cornbread out onto a wire rack to cool.

Remove the giblets from the cavity of the chicken (reserve them if you'll be making gravy). Thoroughly rinse the chicken inside and out. Place it in a stockpot, and cover it with cold water by about 2 inches. Bring the water to a boil. Then reduce the heat to medium-low and simmer for 1 to 1½ hours, or until the chicken is cooked through and tender. Remove the chicken and set aside while preparing the dressing. Reserve the broth.

Preheat the oven to 350°F. Lightly butter a 13 x 9-inch baking pan, and set it aside.

Crumble the cooled cornbread into a large bowl. Melt the butter in a large skillet over medium-high heat. Add the celery, onions, and green onions, and cook until they are tender, 7 to 10 minutes. Then add the mixture to the bowl containing the cornbread. Also add the crumbled white bread, 2½ to 3 cups of the reserved chicken broth, the half-and-half, beaten eggs, salt, sage, and black pepper. Mix everything well to combine. Taste for seasoning. Spoon the dressing mixture into the baking dish. Place the chicken on top of the dressing—either whole or cut in pieces. Return the baking dish to the oven and bake for 25 to 30 minutes, until the chicken is brown on top and the dressing is bubbly around the edges. Remove from the oven and serve immediately.

CITRUS HONEY CHEESECAKE WITH HAZELNUT CRUST

I THINK OF CHEESECAKE as one of those desserts served only on very special occasions. It has always been my youngest brother Chris's favorite. For him, the crust is as important as the cake itself, and it's the crust in this recipe that makes this cheesecake so exceptional. It is made with hazelnuts, and although they might be a bit of a challenge to find, I encourage you not to mess around with substitutes. You won't regret it.

To make the crust, combine the hazelnuts with the sugar and cinnamon in a food processor, and process until as finely chopped as possible—but don't let it turn into a paste. Put the mixture in a small bowl, add the melted butter, and combine well. Press the mixture over the bottom and partially up the sides of a 10-inch springform pan. Set the pan aside.

Preheat the oven to 350°F.

To make the filling, place the cream cheese and sour cream in the bowl of an electric mixer, and beat with the paddle attachment until smooth. Add the honey and beat until there are no lumps. Then add the egg yolks, lemon and orange zests, and vanilla; mix well.

In a large bowl, beat the egg whites until frothy. Gradually add the sugar, beating until the peaks are almost stiff. Stir one third of the egg whites into the cream cheese mixture; then fold in the rest. Pour the batter into the springform pan. Bake on the middle rack of the oven until set just around the edges, 45 to 50 minutes. (Gently shake the pan to test: the cake should be set and not jiggle.) Turn off the oven and leave the cheesecake inside with the door ajar for 2 hours.

Remove the sides from the pan and slide the cheesecake onto a serving plate. Top with chopped hazelnuts, candied orange peel, and slices of kumquats and tangerines. Bring the cake to the table to serve, or cut serving slices for dessert plates.

SERVES 8

FOR THE CRUST
2 cups hazelnuts, toasted and skinned
⅓ cup sugar
½ teaspoon ground cinnamon
8 tablespoons (1 stick) butter, melted

FOR THE FILLING
1½ pounds cream cheese, at room temperature
½ cup sour cream, at room temperature
¾ cup honey
6 eggs, separated, at room temperature
1 tablespoon grated lemon zest
1 tablespoon grated orange zest
1 teaspoon vanilla extract
¼ cup sugar

FOR THE GARNISH
Hazelnuts, toasted, skinned, and chopped
Candied orange peel
Slices of kumquats and tangerines

OLD-FASHIONED BLACKBERRY JAM CAKE

SERVES 8 TO 10

6 eggs, at room temperature

4 cups all-purpose flour

2 teaspoons baking soda

½ teaspoon salt

2 teaspoons ground cinnamon

2 teaspoons ground nutmeg

1 cup black walnuts, chopped

1 cup raisins

2 cups dark brown sugar, packed

1 cup (2 sticks) salted butter, at room temperature

2 cups blackberry jam, at room temperature

2 cups buttermilk, at room temperature

Ma Smith's Caramel Icing (recipe follows)

THIS IS A RECIPE THAT I MODIFIED from one passed down from Margie Hanes Smith, my father's mother. It is a wonderful winter or holiday cake that is a vast improvement over the many fruitcakes that are too often given as gifts this time of the year. I believe this recipe came to her from her mother, my great-grandmother Hanes, who used the blackberry jam as a way to sweeten the cake. Back then sugar was scarce, so jam and sorghum molasses were often used as sweeteners. My family always made our own homemade blackberry jam, so it had seeds, which gave the cake a little extra texture. Recently I made this cake with seedless jam, and I have to say, I missed that crunch. Either way, though, it's a sweet addition.

The recipe also calls for black walnuts, which have their own unique flavor. If you've ever seen black walnuts growing on the tree, you know that in addition to having a very hard shell, they are encased in green husks. If you try to remove the husks by hand, they will stain your fingers with a dark juice that can't be washed off; it has to wear off. So in my childhood we removed the husks by spreading the nuts on the driveway and letting the trucks and tractors run over them. That knocked off the husks, and then came the laborious task of cracking that tough shell to dig out the meat. Happily, today you can buy the nut meats without having to go through all that!

The cake is great with or without the old-fashioned caramel icing. I like it both ways, but without the icing, I usually add a nice big dollop of whipped cream.

Preheat the oven to 325°F. Butter and flour a large tube pan, or use a flour-based baking spray such as Baker's Joy. Set the pan aside.

Separate the eggs, putting the yolks and whites in different mixing bowls. In another large bowl, mix together the flour, baking soda, salt, cinnamon, and nutmeg. In a small bowl, mix ½ cup of the flour mixture with the black walnuts and raisins.

Add the brown sugar, butter, and blackberry jam to the egg yolks, and stir together thoroughly. Stir in the buttermilk. Add the flour mixture.

Beat the egg whites until they turn white but are loose and runny, not too "airy." Fold the egg whites into the batter. Then mix in the nuts and raisins, blending only enough so that they are equally distributed in the batter.

Pour the batter into the tube pan and bake for 1½ to 2 hours. When a toothpick inserted into the center comes out clean, it is done.

Remove the pan from the oven and let the cake cool for about 10 minutes in the pan. Then loosen the cake from the sides of the pan by running a knife around the edge. Invert a cake plate over the pan, and invert the two together. Lift off the tube pan.

Spread the icing smoothly and evenly over the slightly cooled cake. Slice and serve.

MA SMITH'S CARAMEL ICING

MAKES ABOUT 3 CUPS

2 cups dark brown sugar, packed
½ cup heavy cream

8 tablespoons (1 stick) butter, at room temperature

Mix all the ingredients together in a saucepan and cook over medium heat until the sugar has dissolved and the icing is well blended. Remove from the heat. Use while still warm.

BUTTERMILK PECAN PIE

SERVES 8

FOR THE FILLING

8 tablespoons (1 stick) butter, melted

1 ½ cups sugar

3 eggs, beaten

¼ cup all-purpose flour

½ teaspoon salt

1 teaspoon vanilla extract

1 cup buttermilk

1 Easy Pie Crust (page 130), unbaked

Glazed Pecans (recipe follows) chopped, for garnish

NOW, DON'T BE THROWN by the title of this recipe. This is another great "golden oldie" from our family cookbook. Along with roast chicken and mashed potatoes, it is on my short list of favorite comfort foods. Think of it as crème brûlée's culinary cousin. But let me warn you: It's best not to tell your guests the name of the pie before you serve it. As soon as I bring the pie to the table, I can see my guests' eyes light up. But if I say, "Would you like a piece of buttermilk pie?" their expressions darken and I can almost hear them thinking, "Who would make a pie out of buttermilk?" If there are family and friends at the table, they just smile—it means more pie for them.

Preheat the oven to 325°F.

Combine all the filling ingredients in a mixing bowl, and pour the mixture into the unbaked pie shell. Scatter the chopped glazed pecans evenly on top of the pie filling.

Bake for 50 minutes to 1 hour, or until set. Let the pie cool on a wire rack before serving at room temperature.

GLAZED PECANS
MAKES ABOUT 1¼ CUPS

1 cup pecan halves	¼ cup firmly packed light brown sugar	¼ cup dark corn syrup

Preheat the oven to 350°F. Line a jelly-roll pan with aluminum foil, and lightly grease the foil.

Stir the pecan halves, light brown sugar, and dark corn syrup together in a small bowl. Spread the mixture out on the jelly-roll pan, and bake, stirring every 4 minutes, for 12 to 15 minutes, or until the glaze thickens.

Remove the pan from the oven and spread the pecans in a single layer on wax paper. Let the pecans cool completely, separating them with a spoon as they cool. Store the glazed pecans indefinitely in an airtight container at room temperature.

BUCKY'S APRICOT CAKE

MOST OF MY BEST RECIPES have a story about how they came into my possession, and this one is no exception. First, you should know the full name of the person who gave this recipe to me: Buckland Leesberg Farnour III. While that is an impressive moniker, it's a mouthful, so most people just call him Bucky. Years ago, Bucky presented this cake to me and my hardworking landscape crew while we were doing a makeover of his garden. I asked him for the recipe right then and there. It was even better the second time around, and I've made it many times since. It's a delightfully crumbly cake that isn't overly sweet, so it's nice for brunch, too.

P reheat the oven to 350°F. Butter a 10-inch tube pan and dust the bottom and sides with flour, or spray with a flour-based baking spray such as Baker's Joy.

Coarsely chop the apricots and plums. In a small bowl, toss them together with the walnuts to combine. In a medium mixing bowl, sift together the flour, baking powder, baking soda, and salt; set aside.

In another mixing bowl, beat the butter with an electric beater, until fluffy, about 3 minutes. Gradually beat in the sugar and then the eggs, one at a time. Add in the vanilla. Blend in the flour mixture, alternating with the sour cream, beginning and ending with flour. Blend just until the batter is smooth. Gently fold in the plums, apricots, and walnuts.

Using a fork, mix all the streusel ingredients, except the powdered sugar, in a bowl until crumbly.

Spoon one third of the cake batter into the tube pan, spreading it evenly. Sprinkle one third of the streusel mixture over the batter. Repeat, layering the remaining batter and streusel twice. Bake in the oven for 55 to 60 minutes, or until a cake tester comes out clean.

Remove the cake from the oven and let it cool in the pan for about 20 minutes. Run a knife around the inside of the pan to loosen the cake. Invert a cake plate over the pan, and invert the two together. Lift off the tube pan. Sift the powdered sugar over the top, if desired. Slice and serve.

SERVES 8

FOR THE BATTER
¾ cup dried apricots
¾ cup pitted dried plums (prunes)
1 cup chopped walnuts
3 cups all-purpose flour
½ tablespoon baking powder
¾ teaspoon baking soda
¼ teaspoon salt
12 tablespoons (1½ sticks) butter, at room temperature
1½ cups sugar
4 eggs
½ tablespoon vanilla extract
1 cup sour cream

FOR THE STREUSEL
½ cup firmly packed light brown sugar
2 tablespoons butter, at room temperature
2 tablespoons all-purpose flour
1 teaspoon ground cinnamon

2 tablespoons powdered sugar (optional)

HOW TO GROW INGREDIENTS FOR YOUR RECIPES

ENJOYING THE FLAVOR of great-tasting food is one of life's great pleasures. Enhancing your meals with your own homegrown produce makes the food you prepare even better. You can harvest the ingredients at the peak of their freshness and have the assurance that the food is safe and healthy.

I've found the best way to grow vegetables is in framed beds. These are simply bottomless wood boxes that you build on top of the ground and then fill with your own soil mix. There are several benefits to growing your food in a raised bed. First, you can create the right soil mixture. This is especially helpful when the soil around your house isn't ideal. Also, soil in a wooden frame above the surface of the ground warms up faster in the spring, so seeds germinate sooner and roots are stimulated to grow. In the fall, when temperatures drop, you can easily cover the bed and extend the growing season a little longer. A small framed bed is also easier to weed, water, and harvest from than long rows of vegetables.

This plan is for three 8 by 8-foot beds. The size and number of beds you choose to build will depend on your site and your choice of design. Just remember to create beds that are a manageable size: you should be able to reach into the middle of the bed without stepping on the soil. And if you are planning on multiple beds, leave enough space for paths between the frames. I've illustrated various ways the beds can be arranged.

FIRST THINGS FIRST

Before you start constructing the framed beds, there are a few things to do to ensure the success of your garden. The first step is to gather some information.

KNOW YOUR GARDEN'S CLIMATE

Frost Dates

It is important to know when your area usually experiences its last frost in the spring and the first frost in the fall. Since this varies from year to year, the date is an average. Keep in mind that it is a guideline; you need to be aware of weather predictions until the temperatures seem to be stable for several days. For local, reliable advice, contact your area's Cooperative Extension Service or an experienced gardener. The span of time between those dates determines the length of your growing season.

This information helps you plan when to set out your plants. For example, there are some plants, such as cabbage, broccoli, and kale, that can take a light freeze and keep growing, while others, like tomatoes and peppers, will wither and die. For those frost-tender plants, you'll want to make sure you are past the last spring frost date in your area before you put them in the ground. To know which plants can take a frost or need extra protection, check the information on seed packages and plant tags. That's also where you can find out how many days are required for vegetables to grow until they are ready to harvest. That information will help you time the planting of vegetables so they will mature before the estimated date of the first autumn frost.

USDA Hardiness Zones and AHS Heat Zones

If you are planning to grow vegetables that carry over from one year to the next—such as asparagus, strawberries, or fruit trees—you should know your United States Department of Agriculture cold hardiness zone. This will help you determine if a plant will survive the winters in your area. You can find a link to the USDA map on my website PAllenSmith.com, by checking with your local County Extension Service, or by going to www.usna.usda.gov/Hardzone/.

Also, the American Horticultural Society has created a heat tolerance map that indicates the average number of days each year that a given region experiences days with temperatures over 86°F. This information is especially helpful in choosing which plants can best tolerate sustained heat (www.ahs.org/publications/heat_zone_map.htm).

Local Weather Conditions

Gardeners tend to be avid weather watchers, and for good reason. Weather has a direct effect on your plants. Unless you are a meteorologist, it is not likely that you will be able to predict the weather for the coming growing season, but you may be aware of how it has been in the past. For instance, I know that my area often experiences a few days of unseasonably cold weather after the last predicted frost date, which usually comes around Easter. Based on this information I always wait until the first of May, when I know temperatures will stay above freezing, before I put out my tomato transplants.

I also know that a typical summer is hot and humid with minimal amounts of rain. Among other things, this tells me that I need to have a good irrigation system ready and to choose plants that are heat- and drought-tolerant and not prone to fungal problems such as powdery mildew, which thrives in humidity.

If you are not familiar with the weather in your region, check with a neighbor or fellow gardener.

Not only should you inquire about rainfall and temperature, but also ask about violent storms, strong winds, and any other weather conditions that are common to the area.

FIND THE BEST LOCATION FOR YOUR GARDEN

Sunlight

One of the most common mistakes people make is to try to grow vegetables in areas where they don't get enough sunlight. A successful kitchen garden needs at least 6 to 7 hours of direct sun per day. I have found in my own garden that some shade in the late afternoon can be beneficial to my plants. So if you are looking for a site and it has full sun in the morning and most of the day up until the late afternoon, that may be a good location to consider.

Water

A vital element to the success of your garden is keeping your plants well watered. While holding a hose to water your plants may seem like a small chore initially, believe me, by July it gets old in a hurry. Make sure that your kitchen garden is close enough to an outdoor faucet so you can set up an efficient watering system. There are many kinds of innovative watering products available to help you give your plants the water they need to thrive.

I like to use soaker hoses made from recycled tires. The sides are porous and "weep" water through tiny pores throughout the length of the hose. This directs the water to the roots and uses less water than an overhead sprinkler. Soaker hoses also keep the foliage dry, which is important because wet foliage promotes fungal diseases in garden plants. Just snake the soaker hoses about 18 to 20 inches apart through the bed. An easy way to secure them in place is to use U-shaped pins made from wire coat hangers.

New soaker hoses can be hard to straighten out, making them unwieldy and difficult to control. Before you try to place them in your beds, stretch them out in the sun. The heat from the sun will soften them and make them easier to work with.

I also suggest that you get a timer for your watering system. This way you won't have to remember to turn the water on and off. The timer attaches to your outdoor faucet. The best time to water is early in the morning. This allows plants to absorb moisture before the day heats up and also cuts down on fungus problems.

If your region experiences frequent or intermittent rain, it is also good to have a rain gauge on hand to help you determine if your garden needs supplemental moisture. On average, vegetable plants need about $\frac{1}{2}$ to 1 inch of water per week. By keeping an eye on your rain gauge, you can adjust your watering schedule accordingly. Overwatering can be just as damaging as underwatering.

CONSTRUCTING FRAMED BOXES

Once you've found the ideal location for the garden, you are ready to make the frames. I recommend using boards made from a naturally rot-resistant material such as cedar, cypress, or redwood or from engineered materials made from recycled wood and plastics that have the appearance of wood but remain resistant to rot.

Here are the materials you'll need to make three 8 by 8-foot boxes:

- Twelve 8-foot-long boards, 2 inches thick and 12 inches wide
- A box of 1½-inch-long galvanized wood screws
- Thirty-six 2-inch by 2-foot wooden stakes
- Electric drill with wood bits

If you are using a different design, make adjustments to the material list and have the boards cut to the proper length. For this plan, 8-foot-long boards are used to make the boxes. Most building centers have lumber available in that pre-cut length.

Assemble the boxes by making a simple butt joint at each corner, predrilling the holes and then screwing the corners together with galvanized wood screws. Place the box on the ground in the location you've selected. Put a level along the top of the board on each side to make sure the frame is balanced. You may need to dig a small trench under the frame so it sits level on the ground.

Position 2-foot-tall stakes every couple of feet along the inside of the box frame, and hammer them about 1 foot deep into the ground. This will help stabilize the box. You may also wish to attach the stakes to the frame using wood screws. With the frame securely in place, you are ready to add the soil.

FILLING BOXES WITH SOIL

The soil is a critical ingredient to successful gardening. If you don't get the soil right, gardening will be a constant struggle with less than rewarding results. Most vegetable plants are rapid growers and heavy feeders, so they need rich, well-draining soil.

I have heavy clay soil in my garden, which is poor for growing vegetables. I create a blend for my boxes using this formula:

- 50% existing garden soil (heavy clay in my case)
- 25% compost or humus
- 15% well-aged manure
- 10% coarse sand

You can order soil, manure, and compost to be delivered by the cubic yard. A cubic yard covers about 100 square feet, 3 inches deep. For smaller beds you can purchase bagged material at garden and home centers. A 12-inch-deep 8-foot-square box is 64 square feet, so I used a little over 2 cubic yards of soil for each bed. Fill the boxes up to about 2 inches from the top, to leave enough room for a layer of mulch.

Depending on your garden's soil, you may want to create your own mixture. Keep in mind that what you're going for is a healthy, disease-free blend of soil that has plenty of organic matter and drains well. Even if you don't use chemicals or pesticides, you should always wash all the produce you grow to ensure that you are using clean, safe, and great-tasting food.

CHOOSING THE RIGHT PLANTS FOR YOU

Browsing through a seed catalog introduces you to the vast array of vegetables available for planting. For many people, there are so many varieties to choose from that it is hard to decide what to select. Fortunately, there is some basic information that will help narrow the field.

GROWING SEASON

Vegetables can be grouped into two basic categories: cool-season and warm-season varieties. This means that some plants thrive in the cool temperatures of spring or fall (lettuce, peas, cabbage) while others require warm soil and the heat of summer to germinate and develop (corn, tomatoes, cucumbers). Once you identify which of these two groups a vegetable belongs to, you'll know when in the growing season to plant it.

This is important in a raised bed because early spring plants, such as lettuce and radishes, will mature and be finished growing by early summer. They can be removed from the bed and the area where they were growing can be planted with a warm-season vegetable. I've illustrated how that idea works below.

FOOD YOU CAN GROW IN THREE 8 X 8-FOOT FRAMED BED GARDENS

As vegetables grow and are harvested, new varieties can be planted in their place, providing you with three seasons of fresh produce. Here's a schedule of recommended plants.

EARLY SPRING PLANTING

BED 1: Goosefoot and Onion family

'Rainbow Lights' Swiss chard
'Spinner' spinach
'Tyee' spinach
'Tall Top Early Wonder' beets
'Organic Evergreen Bunching' green onions

BED 2: Brassica and Onion family

'Bonnie Hybrid' cabbage
'Premium Crop' broccoli
Arugula
'Hakurei' turnips
Green bunching onions
'French Breakfast' radishes

BED 3: Sunflower, Legume, Onion, and Carrot family

'Red Sails' lettuce
'Parris Island Cos' romaine lettuce
'Sugar Anne' snap peas
'Red Cored Chantenay' carrots
'Harris Model' parsnips
'Giant Musselburgh' leeks

SUMMER PLANTING

BED 1: Gourd family

'Black Beauty' zucchini squash
'Early Prolific Straightneck' squash
'Straight Eight' cucumbers

BED 2: Nightshade and Mint family

'Celebrity' tomato
'Black Beauty' eggplant
'Bonnie Bell' peppers
Red bell peppers
'Lettuce Leaf' basil

BED 3: Carrot, Onion, and Legume family

'Harris Model' parsnips (from spring)

'Giant Musselburgh' leeks (from spring)

'Fernleaf' dill

'Bush Blue Lake 274' bush beans or 'Royal Burgundy' bush beans

FALL PLANTING

BED 1: Brassica and Onion family

'Savoy Ace' cabbage

'Early Dividend' broccoli

'Winterbor' kale

Mesclun gourmet greens

'Cherry Belle' radishes

'He shi ko' bunching (green) onions

BED 2: Sunflower, Carrot, Onion, and Legume family

'Buttercrunch' Bibb lettuce

'Granada' leaf lettuce

'Brune d'Hiver' lettuce

Curly parsley

'Little Marvel' peas

'Scarlet Nantes' carrots

'American Flag' leeks

BED 3: Goosefoot, Onion, and Carrot family

'Harris Model' parsnips (from spring)

'Giant Musselburgh' leeks (from spring)

'Ruby' Swiss chard

'Correnta' spinach

'Bloomsdale Long Standing' spinach

'Cylindra' beets

It's worth the time to look for each plant's individual characteristics, such as frost tolerance, days to maturity, and whether it is an annual (lives for one growing season) or a perennial (returns the following year without replanting). Knowledge will give you planting prowess in the gardening world! Here's more information that may help.

HYBRIDS VS. OPEN POLLINATION

Hybrid vegetables are varieties that have been created by cross-pollination with the help of plant breeders rather than natural open pollination. Many people like the new improved qualities of hybrids, but open-pollinated plants have advantages, too. One of the perks of open-pollinated vegetables is that their seeds will produce plants that are identical to the parents, whereas seeds from a hybrid plant will not reproduce as predictably. If you are a seed collector, that may be important. Experiment to discover what works best for you. On many plant tags or seed packets you will see the variety is an F1 hybrid. This means it is a first-generation hybrid and should be a vigorous grower with good yields.

ALL AMERICAN SELECTIONS

When you see a red, white, and blue shield on a seed packet or plant tag, it signifies that the variety is an All American Selection award winner. This means it has been tested in trial gardens and found to be an outstanding performer for home gardens. AAS awards are given to vegetables, flowers, and bedding plants. You can find AAS award-winning varieties that were introduced as far back as 1933. AAS varieties are a good choice because they are likely to be successful in a wide range of conditions.

To help you along in your plant selections, I've listed some of my favorites.

Luscious Lettuces

'Red Sails'

'Buttercrunch'

'Black Seeded Simpson'

'Granada'

'Tom Thumb'

'Jericho'

'Saladbowl'

'Limestone'

'Rouge d'Hiver'

'Parris Island'

'Deer Tongue'

Great Garden Herbs

Cilantro

Flat-leaf (Italian) parsley

Curly parsley

Bouquet dill

'Fernleaf' dill

'Salem' rosemary

Prostrate rosemary

'African Blue' basil

'Lettuce Leaf' basil

'Purple Ruffles' basil

Onion chives

Thyme

Tasty Heritage Tomato Varieties

'Mortgage Lifter'

'Pruden's Purple'

'Cherokee Purple'

'Amish Paste'

'Brandywine'

'Aunt Ruby's German Green'

'San Marzano' paste

'Black Krim'

'Lemony', aka 'Limmony'

'Abe Lincoln'

SQUEEZED FOR SPACE?

Here are some vegetable varietals that can be grown in containers. Use large pots that have drainage holes and fill them with bagged potting soil.

Tomatoes: 'Balconi Red' and 'Balconi Yellow', 'Husky Cherry Red', 'Celebrity' or 'Celebrity Bush', Roma

Eggplant: 'Ichiban' or 'Early Long Purple'

Snap peas: 'Sugar Snap' or 'Sugar Anne'

Swiss chard: 'Rainbow Lights' or 'Ruby Red'

Peppers: 'Mini Bell Mix,' Red Knight, habanero

Zucchini squash: 'Black Beauty'

Cucumber: 'Burpless Bush' or 'Spacemaster' (provide trellis for support)

Lettuce: any kind

Carrots: 'Little Finger'

Kale

AREAS WITH A SHORT GROWING SEASON

If you live in a cool northern climate, here are a few tips that will help you grow warm-season favorites that require more than 60 days from seed to harvest, such as tomatoes.

- Get a head start by selecting large plants rather than sowing seeds.
- Grow vegetables in containers on casters so they can easily be moved indoors in case of late spring or early fall frost.
- Select plant varieties with early maturity dates, such as 'Early Girl' tomatoes, which mature in 52 days.

MAINTENANCE

MULCH

A good way to retain moisture and keep the soil temperature even and the weeds under control is to apply a 2- to 3-inch layer of mulch after the ground warms in the spring and the plants emerge. Although ground or shredded bark is most common, there are many types of materials that can be used as mulch, such as grass clippings, seed hulls, even landscape cloth. If available, straw is another possibility because it is relatively free of weed seeds. It works especially well as a path material between your framed beds because it is slow to decay. Check for bales at farmers' co-ops. Straw should be applied in a thin, even layer and checked frequently for snails and slugs because they like it, too.

WILDLIFE CONTROL

One of the heartbreaks of vegetable gardening is discovering that all your hard work has been looted by the local wildlife. Now, depending on the severity of the damage and the persistence of the pests, some people find repellents such as bars of soap, bags of hair, or commercial products helpful. Others find that once an animal realizes that such an object is not going to do it any harm, or the commercial repellents wash away, they become ineffective.

An alternative is behavior modification. Simple electric fencing works well if you do not have children or pets. Another approach is to set up a motion-activated sprinkler. The animals get blasted with a shot of water when they enter your garden. But if your kitchen garden is repeatedly invaded by foraging animals, the best solution is to enclose it with a fence.

For deer, the fence needs to be at least 8 feet tall and constructed of a heavy-gauge wire. If room allows, I also suggest planting a hedge of deer-resistant shrubs (check with local nurseries for varieties they recommend for your area) about 4 feet away from the outside perimeter of the fence. Deer are excellent vertical jumpers, but they cannot cover much ground in a single jump, so the hedge will prevent them from leaping over the fence.

A shorter fence can be used if the wildlife is smaller, such as rabbits. Just be sure to select a material that they cannot slip through. To keep out burrowing animals, bury the fence into the ground about 2 feet below the surface.

ACKNOWLEDGMENTS

THIS COOKBOOK REQUIRED the talents and dedication of so many: shoppers, gatherers, vegetable harvesters, dish washers, and tasters.

My thanks all of those who worked tirelessly at preparing the food for testing and tasting: Teri Bunce, Ray Bunce, Tas Lehocky, Victoria Gross, Marlea Mestra, and Amanda Wells.

Additionally I would like to thank those that were front and center with the food styling and organizing of the photo shoots: Sheb Fisher, Jamie Kim, and Chip Jones.

I am grateful to our photographer, Ben Fink, for his talented eye and great sense of humor throughout the photo shoots. I thank Jane Colclasure and Kelly Quinn for their contributions to the photographs here and in the entire Garden Home series.

I extend my gratitude to our entire publications team—Betsy Lyman, for helping keep us on track and working so diligently on the manuscript, and Suzanne Selby, for keeping up with the photos and recipes. This project involved the support of the entire Hortus production family: David Curran, Cindy Alpe, Brent Walker, Kevin Waltermire, Mary Ellen Pyle, Pam Holden, Stewart McLendon, Todd Orr, Bill Rech, Laura Leech, Betty Freeze, Mimi San Pedro, Brandi Moran, Caleb Rash, and Patrick Green.

Our design team made the gardens beautiful for the cameras. I thank Ward Lile, Nicole Claas-Moore, Sarah Burr, Lorri Davis, and Mary Talbot.

My friends in the culinary world were great fun to work with, and I am grateful for their support: Chef Lee Richardson, Capi Peck Petersen, Peter Brave, and Regina Charboneau.

My gratitude also extends to my wonderful friends and family who have been a constant support and offered their talents toward this book, the Garden Home series, and other related endeavors: Susan, Rich, Graceleigh and Sawyer Wright, Herren and Susan Hickingbotham, Mark and Laura Doramus, Kent Holt, Julie Thompson, Sondra and Todd Quick, Sheb and Danny Fisher, Laura and James Leech, Ken and Ellen Hughes, Rick Smith and Susan Sims Smith, Brian Hardin, Warren and

Harriet Stephens, Carl Miller, Jr., Claiborne and Elaine Deming, Kim and Mark Brockinton, Cheri and Mark Nichols, Jim Dyke and Helen Porter, Janice Goodwin, Reed and Rebecca Thompson, Kellie Mills, Gaye and Robert Anderson, Henry and Marilyn Lile, Doug Buford, Kathy Graves, members of the Little Rock Garden Club, Stephen Christenson, Robert and Mary Lynn Dudley, Jay and Patsy Hill, Bob and Marilyn Bogle, David Paul Garner, Jr., and the Marlsgate Plantation, Fred and Margaret Carl, Daisy Garner, Capital Hotel, Ashley's Restaurant, Antha Smith Keyt, Valerie Dodd, Edwina Mann, Ed and Pat Matthews, Terry and Cathy Getha, Frank Reese, Bob Swain, Bob and Barbara Hopp, Chip Jones, Scott Lile, Rusty and Judy Evans, Joe and Jamie Foster, Twin Oaks, Monmouth Plantation, Ravenna, and the staff at the Capital Hotel.

This book is very much about the garden, and without the work of so many, this would not have been possible. The farm and garden crews stepped in to always lend a hand: Chris and Joyce Smith, Luis Gonzales, Ricky Sanchez, Wes Parsons, Josh Lindsey, Antonio Cruz, Francisco Ramirez, Jose Sanchez, and Ricky Morris.

My gratitude also extends to the many companies that have been instrumental in their support: ABC Carpet and Home, Ag-Pro Companies, Anthropologie, Jason Garner of Antique Brick Company, B.A. Framer, Benjamin Moore, Bennett Brothers Stone Company, Bonnie Plant Farms, Boulevard Bread Company, Brea Water, Circa Lighting, Classic Marble and Granite, Conard Pyle, Crown Point Cabinetry, Cynthia East Fabrics, Dawn Solar, Euro American, Ferry Morse Seed Company, Follansbee, Four Star Greenhouse, Garden Safe, GJ Styles, Global Views, Green Circle, Susan Henry of Cobblestone and Vine, Hickory Chair, Homespice Décor, J. Poker and Sons, Jiffy Products, John Deere, Just Add Ice Orchids, Kohler, Laneventure, Lee Industries, Lennox, Lennox Hearth, Marvin Windows, Merida Meridian, Michaelian Home, Mountain Valley Water, Oly, Pleasant View Gardens, Premier Horticultural Soil, Pro-Mix, Proven Winners, Quail Valley Grasses, Rainbird, Restoration Tile, Spectrum, Stihl, Subaru, Sunbrella, Timberlane, Tri-B Nurseries, Trio's, Up Country Living, Vagabond, Van Bloom, Van Zyverden, Viking Range Corporation, Walpole Woodworkers, Whole Foods, Wildseed Farms, Williams-Sonoma.

Certainly this project would not have been a reality without the deft talents of the entire Clarkson Potter staff working together as a team. They made the book sing with all their sound advice on the narratives, recipes, and layout: Emily Takoudes, Peggy Paul, Doris Cooper, Mark McCauslin, Kathie Ness, Joan Denman, Jane Treuhaft, Stephanie Huntwork, Kate Tyler, and Lauren Shakely.

INDEX

Note: Page references in *italics* refer to photographs.